MAYNE ISLAND

& THE OUTER GULF ISLANDS
A HISTORY

by Marie Elliott

Gulf Islands Press, Mayne Island, B.C.

Cover photograph by Cyrus Dean
Back photograph by Robert Elliott
Maps 1 and 3 by Diana Hocking, Victoria

Typesetting by ATS Typesetting Services, Victoria
Printed by Fleming Printing Ltd., Victoria
Published by Gulf Islands Press
    Box 79, Mayne Island, B.C. V0N 2J0

Canadian Cataloguing in Publication Data

Elliott, Marie
    Mayne Island and the Outer Gulf Islands, a History

Includes index
    ISBN 0-9691674-0-7

PREFACE

I am the fortunate descendant of two pioneer families of Mayne Island, the Thomas Bennetts and the William Collinsons, but I learned at an early age that along with a sense of pride, pioneer heritage carries with it a measure of accountability, too. Repeat once too often the anecdotes handed down from generation to generation and you become suspected of telling less than the truth.

This book began, therefore, as a simple attempt to verify the old stories — and to save a few reputations. Eventually, I gathered enough material to write an M.A. thesis for the University of Victoria, and, now, after five years of research the time seems right to share with you what has been learned so far. I have placed Mayne Island at the hub of historical development in the Gulf Islands because that is where the island seems to have remained, from the earliest times until the present. After completing further research, I hope to examine the early history of North and South Pender, Galiano and Saturna in greater detail in a future planned volume.

There are many people to thank, for even the briefest interview yielded a gem of information that made my task lighter. Regretfully, I must limit names, but I trust those people whose names have been omitted will forgive me. My two most important assistants were my parents Fred and Margaret Bennett, who have carefully treasured in memories and material evidence the early history of Mayne Island, and have patiently encouraged my research and writing. A second major source of support and information were the descendants of the early settlers on Mayne and the other Islands: Caroline Hopton, Wilbert and John Deacon, Vera Greene, Gordon Robson, Mary Ellen Harding, Kathleen Garrick, Ellen Adams, John and Anna DeRousie, Eve Grey Smith, Gertrude Vigurs, Edith Higginbottom, Elsie Arnet and John Bennett. For the twentieth century history of Mayne Island, Robert Aitken, Jack Borradaile, Jesse and Elsie Brown, Kay Carpenter, Frank Cotton, Reg Cousens, Fred Dodds, Bertha Evans, Fred Flick, Dick and Roland Foster, Amelia Georgeson, Foye Miles, Bill and Marguerite Morson, John Nagata, Mabel Nicholson, Mildred Page, Nancy Rainsford, Peter Roberts and Bill and Elsie Wilks provided important material and inspiration. Our Mayne Island representatives on the Islands Trust in 1983, Joan Sprague and Ed Williams, were generous with their time and advice.

All the municipal, provincial, and federal government offices contacted during my research were most cooperative, especially the staff of the Provincial Archives, Legislative Library, Islands Trust, Capital Regional District, Ministry of Transportation and Highways, and Legal Surveys, in Victoria. Mark Walsh, Hudson's Bay Company Archives, Winnipeg; David A Smith, Public Archives of Canada, Ottawa; David Jones, C.P.R. Archives, Montreal; and R. Garth Walker, Anglican Provincial Synod of British Columbia Archives, Vancouver, saved me considerable time and expense.

For their pioneering efforts in photography, I am indebted to Cyrus Dean for the early photograph of Springwater Lodge and Miners Bay used on the cover of this book; to John (Jack) Aitken for his excellent record of buildings and social life on Mayne Island between 1905 and 1920; and to Mabel Foster for continuing this record from 1920 to 1950.

This book rests on the foundation laid by members of the Gulf Island Branch of the British Columbia Historical Association (now Federation), who collected and published the early stories of the Gulf Island pioneers in *A Gulf Islands Patchwork* (1961), edited by Captain and Mrs. Claxton, and Beatrice J. Freeman.

I shall always be grateful for the patient criticism and advice of Dr. James E. Hendrickson, Department of History, University of Victoria, who supervised my graduate thesis and encouraged its publication.

The Mayne Island Agricultural Society kindly provided a grant for research; the British Columbia Heritage Trust and the British Columbia Historical Federation provided publication assistance.

Marie Elliott,
Mayne Island,
January 1984.

TABLE OF CONTENTS

LIST OF MAPS

For my parents, Fred and Margaret Bennett, my children, Robert and Carol, and everyone who considers the Gulf Islands of British Columbia a special paradise.

INTRODUCTION

A dramatic confrontation between country and city is occurring all over North America today as rural communities face the threat of urban assimilation. There is an urgent need for historians to define these vulnerable rural areas before they vanish from the maps. One of the most threatened sectors in British Columbia lies in Georgia Strait, midway between the province's two largest metropolitan regions, Vancouver and Victoria. Despite the insularity provided by a marine environment, the southern Gulf Islands, comprised of Salt Spring, and the outer islands of North and South Pender, Saturna, Galiano and Mayne, are rapidly becoming part of the Georgia Strait urban region.

From the earliest settlement period until the present, Mayne Island's history is a prime example of a marine community that had to come to terms with its vulnerable location in southern Georgia Strait. The island became the social hub of the outer Gulf Islands because of several natural advantages, and while the residents dealt with the problems of establishing and maintaining a rural community in close proximity to the mainland, they made a unique contribution to the development of the province.

Local history provides an opportunity to examine closely the lives of individuals in order to discover how much they adapted to their environment, and how much of the environment was changed to suit their needs. The extent of these adaptations on Mayne Island is illustrated by studies of individuals from each major time period, i.e., early settlement, 1900 to 1960, and 1960 to 1980. The studies are also used to illustrate the social conditions of the island residents. Was the nature of Mayne Island egalitarian? Closely-knit?

British Columbia historians tend to overlook small, rural communities when tracing the development of the province. The nineteenth-century history of British Columbia concentrates on the Cariboo gold rush and the growth of Vancouver and Victoria. It seldom questions what happened to the ex-gold miners once they were ready to become settlers, nor the contributions made by their families. These early pioneers established many of the small agricultural settlements in British Columbia before a large number of middle-class British immigrants arrived in the late nineteenth century, yet the latter receive the praise for introducing a civilizing influence. Native-white relationships is another area that has been largely ignored, especially the subject of Indian wives, who were a stabilizing factor in their partnerships with white settlers. At a later stage in

British Columbia history, the contribution of the Japanese, and their acceptance in society has been chiefly defined by the negative evidence of racial discrimination. Mayne Island's social development provides a positive aspect to the history of the Japanese in British Columbia, together with challenging new information about Indian wives and ex-gold miners.

With a favorable economy in the 1950's and 1960's, British Columbia's population and industries expanded rapidly, and the rural areas became much more vulnerable for exploitation. The Mayne Island community at first wanted to become part of this development, but later had difficulty coping with the demands placed on its land resources. The legislation of the Islands Trust by the provincial government in 1974 was a major experiment in local government and environmental control for the entire Gulf Island region, extending as far north as Denman and Hornby Islands.

The history of Mayne Island and the outer Gulf Islands demonstrates that an examination of rural communities in British Columbia can be richly rewarding. Details about the social, economic and political development of the island help to fill in the larger, over-all picture of our province's past, and present new evidence for social historians concerned with our ethnic heritage, and for environmentalists and land planners concerned with the effects of future population demands.

MAP No. 1

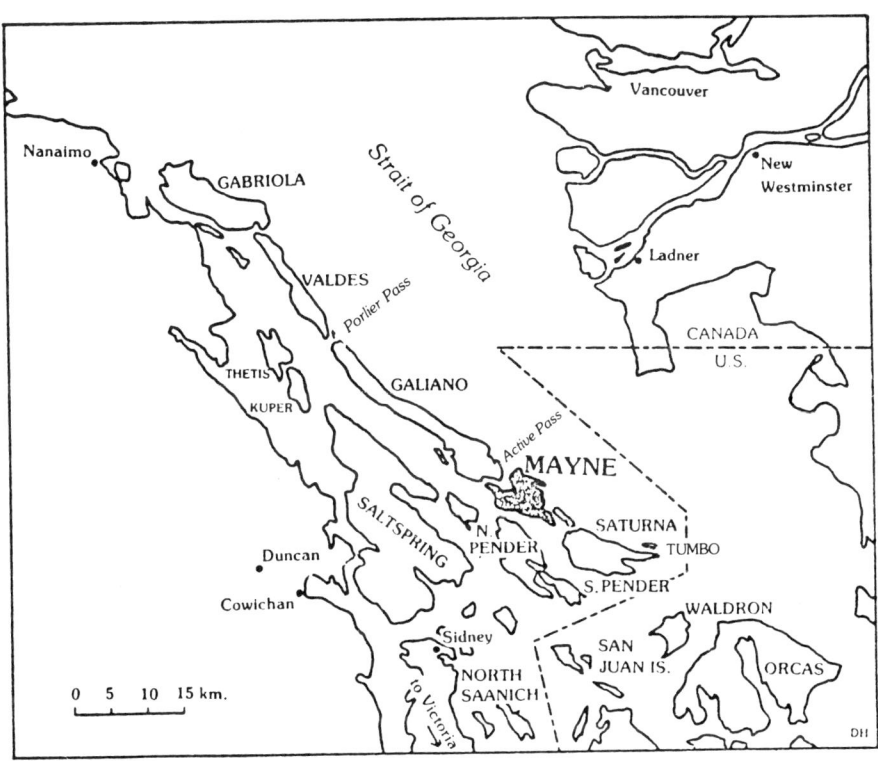

The Southern Gulf Islands of British Columbia

x

Antler pendant, collected from beach below midden site at Helen Point, Mayne Island (2.3 × 1.4 × 0.2 centimetres). On display at B. C. Provincial Museum, Victoria. B. C. Provincial Museum photo.

Anthropomorphic carving of antler, collected from beach below midden at Helen Point, Mayne Island (4.3 × 2.7 × 0.5 centimetres). Probably 200 years old. On display at B. C. Provincial Museum, Victoria. B. C. Provincial Museum photo.

1

BEGINNINGS

The sea gave birth to Mayne Island some forty million years ago, and has dominated the history of the island ever since, carving out valleys and shore indentations during post glacial periods, providing sustenance for the earliest native Indian inhabitants, challenging the efforts of intrepid settlers to establish homesteads, and paradoxically threatening isolation while enhancing a utopian ideal.

With a surface area of 5,750 acres, Mayne Island is the second smallest, populated island of the southern Gulf Island group that also includes Galiano, Saturna, Salt Spring, and North and South Pender Islands (see map page ix). The southern Gulf Islands are an extension of the San Juan archipelago and lie midway between Vancouver Island and the mainland in southern Georgia Strait. During the Late Cretaceous period, approximately 100 million years ago, this region was established by sedimentary deposition in the Nanaimo Basin, which extended from Sucia Island in Washington State northwest to Nanoose Bay on Vancouver Island.[1]

Tectonic activity 40 million years ago thrust this deposition into anticlines with axial planes trending northwest/southeast. Subsequent breeching, erosion, faulting, igneous intrusions (on Salt Spring only), glacial activity and marine incursions created islands with low valleys of silt-covered shale, and rocky, barren cuestas of impervious conglomerate. Thus, the valleys contain soil that is fertile and productive, whereas the hillsides are suitable for limited grazing purposes only.[2]

Mayne Island possesses a greater percentage of agricultural land than most of the outer Islands. Three fertile valleys that bisect the island from northwest to southeast provided farm sites for the early settlers. A mild climate, averaging 2,000 hours of sunshine and 31 inches of rain annually, was also conducive to settlement and agricultural production.[3]

The island's physical location on the south side of Active Pass, with a large harbour, Miners Bay, midway through the waterway, was an asset for two reasons. Isolation, always a major factor to contend with in island living, was reduced when steam vessels used the Pass after 1855 as part of the shortest route between Victoria and the mainland. Secondly, large quantities of salmon migrated through the Pass to the Fraser River, providing sustenance and income from fishing.[4]

Indian women at Miners Bay. Although photographed in the 1920's, this scene could have greeted the Spanish explorers and the early settlers. Mabel Foster photo.

Archaelogical evidence has placed man on Mayne Island as early as 3000 B.C. when forerunners of the Nanaimo and Cowichan Indian tribes, Halkomelem speakers, used Helen Point at the south entrance to Active Pass as a fishing station. More recently, Straits Salish (Songhees, Saanich) temporarily used the same site, trapping fish in large reef nets. Three distinct cultural phases have been established: Mayne, Marpole and San Juan, the latter dating from 1200 A.D. to European contact.[5]

The Spanish found Indians residing on Galiano during explorations in 1791 and 1792, and they were probably present on the other Islands as well. The *Sutil* and *Mexicana,* under Commanders Don Dionisio Galeano and Don Cayetano Valdez, anchored overnight in June 1792 in a bay off the east coast of Galiano Island that the Spaniards named Anclage. While navigating the strong tides of Porlier Pass the next day they encountered "healthy-looking young men and two older men" who offered bramble berries, shellfish and water in return for beads and buttons. The Spaniards found these natives to be more "trusting and affable" than those encountered later at Nanaimo.[6]

Sixty years later, when the Royal Navy commenced surveying the coasts of Vancouver Island and the mainland in 1858, they observed Indians residing on Mayne Island. The earliest detailed maps of the area, prepared by Captain George Henry Richards, show an Indian village at Mayne Island on a bay named, rather unimaginatively, Village Bay.[7] On March 3, 1877, the Joint Reserve Committee designated the land at Helen Point, Mayne Island, as an Indian reserve.[8] Whereas elsewhere in the province many of the reserves established by the Committee were not recognized, this particular reserve of 323 acres has remained intact and occupied by members of the Cowichan tribe to the present day. Thus, descendants of the first Indian tribes to occupy Helen Point three thousand years ago were on Mayne Island to assist the first white settlers when they arrived in 1861.

Captain George Henry Richards and Mrs. Richards with the crew of HMS Plumper. Seated (l to r) Sub-lieutenant E. P. Bedwell; Ship's Doctor, Surgeon David Lyell; Mrs. Richards; and 1st Lieutenant William Moriarty. Standing (l to r) Lieutenant Daniel Pender; W. H. J. Brown, paymaster; Captain Richards; and 2nd Lieutenant R. C. Mayne. PABC 33711

* * * * *

When Governor James Douglas made a canoe trip from Victoria through the "Canal de Arro" to visit the coal district at Wentuhuysen Inlet (Nanaimo) in 1852, he found his maps extremely inaccurate, with the coastline of Vancouver Island charted fifteen to twenty miles east of where it should be, and the "intermediate space" occupied by islands that he named the Arro Archipelago. In a paper read before the Royal Geographical Society in London, Douglas recommended that this region be surveyed as soon as possible in order that merchant ships plying between Victoria and Wentu-huysen Inlet could use a shorter route than the existing one by way of Georgia Strait.[9] This survey was not carried out until 1858-59 by Captain George Henry Richards on the survey ship H.M.S. *Plumper.* Many of the Gulf Islands had been named during the voyages of the early Spanish explorers and Captain George Vancouver in 1791 and 1792, but Mayne Island was designated by Captain Richards to honor his lieutenant on the *Plumper,* Richard Charles Mayne. Upon his return to England in 1862, Mayne published *Four Years in British Columbia and Vancouver Island,* which has become a classic account of conditions in early British Columbia.[10]

At the same time that Richards was surveying the southern Georgia Strait region, the first white occupation of Mayne Island commenced in 1858 when gold miners, en route to the Fraser River from Victoria, began stopping overnight at what soon became known as Miners Bay, Plumper Pass (see map page 11). Two freshwater streams and a relatively flat camping area adjacent to a gravel beach made the area an attractive resting place. Plumper Pass was the name first used for Active Pass by the local settlers, a practice that continued into the twentieth century. In his book, Mayne hints that Active Pass was originally called Plumper Pass.[11] Captain Richards officially named the waterway Active Pass in 1858 upon learning that the U.S.S. *Active,* which had assisted Richards in surveying Semiahmoo Bay in connection with the international boundary dispute, had been the first naval steamship to use the Pass in 1855.[12] Nevertheless, local usage persisted. The first post office to serve the outer Gulf Islands, located at Miners Bay, was called Plumper Pass in 1880, and the Provincial Police lockup, built near the post office in 1896, bore the Plumper Pass designation. The post office officially changed its name to Mayne Island on April 1, 1900, but as late as 1909 journalists were still writing articles for the newspapers using Plumper Pass to describe the Active Pass area.[13]

The first settlers to record pre-emptions in the Plumper Pass region chose Miners Bay and the valley running eastward from it across the island, about 1861.[14] Their diverse backgrounds represented the wide variety of newcomers to British Columbia at the time of the Cariboo gold rush. Christian Mayers was of German descent, a native of Plochingen in the kingdom of Wurttemberg, and James Messenger Greavy came from Boston, Massachusets, and before that from New Brunswick.[15] They each registered 100-acre tracts of land, the size of the lots surveyed in the Cowichan and Nanaimo districts in 1859.[16] Optimistically calling their farming area New Brighton, they pro-ceeded to establish small ranches stocked with cattle and hogs.[17] Greavy and Mayers may also have cut cedar shingles and salmon cask staves. German settlers on Salt

Spring Island received $3.50 per 1000 shingles in Victoria in 1860.[18]

Creating a homestead on Mayne Island was somewhat less arduous for Mayers and Greavy than for settlers in other parts of British Columbia where terrain and climate were more forbidding. Cedar, alder and fir trees comprised a large proportion of the timber on their pre-emptions, providing fuel for heating, and durable building materials for homes, outbuildings and split-rail fences. Without expensive saws, the easiest method to clear land was to bore holes with an auger into the centers of the large fir and cedar trees, then fill the holes with hot coals. The process was repeated, once the trees were felled, to eliminate them altogether.[19]

Access to the growing communities of New Westminster, Nanaimo and Victoria was readily available by boat. Each place, approximately thirty miles away, required a day and a half travelling time if a sail was employed and advantage taken of the tides, which tend to flow south on the ebb and north on the flood.[20] Mayers and Greavy acquired a small sloop, the *General Hancock,* in order to transport farm produce and cattle to city markets.[21]

* * * * *

The first major difficulty for the settlers to overcome was not hewing a homestead from the forest but dealing with the Indians, for their reaction to the settlers was an unknown factor. Not only did local resident Indians outnumber the settlers[22] but renegade bands roamed the waterways from the San Juan Islands north to Kuper Island. The Cowichan Indians were known to have used the narrow passages through Plumper Pass and Porlier Pass as convenient locations for plundering the canoes of other tribes.[23] Added to this uneasy situation was the knowledge that the Haidas made trading visits to Victoria, spurning the seasonal, northern trading trips of the Hudson's Bay Company ships *Labouchere* and *Otter.*[24] While both white and Negro settlers on Salt Spring Island had experienced their violence, it appears that Mayne Island residents were spared.[25] Nevertheless, a least three incidents involving white-Indian conflict have been documented for the Plumper Pass area.

In 1863 Christian Mayers invited Frederick Marks, a fellow countryman, living with his wife and five children on Waldron Island, to join him at Miners Bay. On April 8 Mayers and Marks set out in two boats to move the family's effects to Mayne Island. Mayers reached Miners Bay safely with Mrs. Marks and four of the children, but Frederick Marks and his young, married daughter, Caroline Harvey, were murdered by members of a renegade Lamalcha band as they camped overnight on Saturna Island. In reporting the murder to authorities in Victoria, Mayers stated that he had never before experienced any difficulty from the Cowichan Indians on Mayne Island and had one member in his employ. According to the Victoria *Colonist,* the future settlement of the Islands was in jeopardy:

Mr. Mayer [sic] states that formerly he used to travel in his boat without either gun or knife, but that now even armed and with companions he feels alarmed lest himself may be a victim in the next tragedy. Mrs. Marks and family, who were left at Plumper's Pass [sic] under the care of one man, were in much distress and terror when our informant left. Of late there have been numerous farms pre-empted on the islands lying between Plumper Pass and San Juan; there will, however, be an end to all settlement if effective measures are not promptly taken for giving the necessary protection to isolated residents, and terminating the "reign of terror" which seems to have been inaugurated.[26]

The spring of 1863 was an especially difficult time for white-Indian relations. Besides the murder of Marks and his daughter, William Brady was killed and his companion, John Henley, wounded by Indians at Bedwell Harbour, Pender Island. Further north, Indians attacked white traders at Bentinck Arm.[27] Concerned that London might misinterpret the alarmist stance of the Victoria newspapers, Douglas hastened to inform the Duke of Newcastle, Colonial Secretary, that only a few Indians were involved; there was no threat of a general uprising among the native population. James Douglas had been under pressure by the residents of Salt Spring Island for some time to provide them with law enforcement on that island. These incidents were enough to force him to appoint John Peter Mouat Biggs as Justice of the Peace for Salt Spring in May 1863.[28]

After more than a month of investigation by the Victoria police, aided by the Royal Navy gunboats *Forward, Grappler, Cameleon* and *Devastation,* during which time one seaman was killed and the Indian village on Kuper Island razed in an act of "forest diplomacy," the murderers of Marks and Brady were apprehended. They were tried, convicted and executed at public hangings in May and July 1863. The executions were witnessed by friends and relatives of the Indians.[29]

At the time that Mayers reported the Marks and Harvey slayings, he stated that an Indian in his employ had talked about the murder of three white men at Plumper Pass in 1858, perpetrated by a "certain bad Indian" who liked to boast of his exploits in killing white men.[30] On the evidence of two witnesses an elderly Indian named Skul-a-weet was found guilty of murdering an unnamed white man on an unnamed island about five years previous to July 1863, but lack of further information prevents linking the island with Mayne Island.[31]

In the summer of 1870, a further incident involving Indians and Plumper Pass settlers occurred. Robert Clarke had given up a tinker's existence in Victoria to attempt homesteading with his wife Annie and three children at Village Bay. While Annie was away overnight with her children visiting Sophie Georgeson on Galiano Island, Clarke was shot and killed as he split cedar shakes near his home, and his cabin was looted.[32] The local settlers immediately sent a request to the Colonial Secretary in Victoria for a gunboat to "teach the Indians a lesson," but the request was denied on the grounds that the Indians involved might not belong to the Gulf Island tribes.[33] Police Commissioner Augustus F. Pemberton posted a $500 reward for the apprehension of the murderer, which was not achieved until after a month of investigation by Victoria and New Westminster police.[34]

The jury was unable to reach a verdict during the first trial, but evidence presented before Judge Matthew Baillie Begbie during the second trial in November 1870 indicated that an Indian named Tom had been seeking revenge for the ill-treatment received from a Portuguese settler on Galiano a few days before the murder. Although a second jury found Tom guilty, and Judge Begbie sentenced the man to death, execution was delayed for more than two years by petitions from Tom's friends.[35]

Troubles with the Indians continued at least until 1873 when Tom was finally executed. In September 1871 a petition signed by fifteen settlers at Plumper Pass requested the appointment of a local constable because the Indians were becoming "very toublesome and saucy, and they openly threaten to kill a white man."[36] On May 6, 1873, Henry Georgeson returned from Victoria to find his wife unconscious on the floor of their home. He claimed that the Indians had tried to poison Sophie, possibly in revenge for his testimony at the trial of Indian Tom.[37]

Oldtimers of the Plumper Pass region maintain that their great-grandfathers deliberately chose Indian wives in order to protect themselves and their homesteads. In disputes with the Indians, these women would act as mediators. The difficulties experienced by the Clarkes and Georgesons contradict this belief and suggest an opposite conjecture: that white-native relationships may have been viewed with antagonism by the Indians. Despite their Indian status Annie Clarke and Sophie Georgeson were both victims of native retaliation.[38]

Demographic evidence on the Gulf Islands refutes another recent theory about Indian wives. Robin Fisher has argued that "An Indian wife was a positive advantage to a fur trader but not to a settler. Some settlers did form temporary liaisons with Indian women but more commonly they provided merely a temporary satisfaction of desires."[39] Most of the sixteen settlers at the northeast settlement on Salt Spring Island in 1860 had Indian wives,[40] as did six of the earliest settlers in the Plumper Pass district: Christian Mayers, Henry Georgeson, Robert Clarke, Jacob Heck, John Silva and William T. Collinson. Native women were trained from birth to live in the wilderness, a factor that added stability to their relationships with white men, especially during the early stages of establishing a homestead. With the possible exception of Mayers, all of the Plumper Pass unions were permanent until the death of one of the partners.[41] This evidence suggests that a study of other rural districts in British Columbia might also yield similar information regarding lifetime parterships between white settlers and Indian women.

When the Thomas Bennett family arrived on Mayne Island in 1879 there was still one elderly Indian living near their homestead, located three miles from the Indian reserve. The only difficulties they encountered with the Indians were the occasional potato raids carried out by the Tsawwassen band, residing directly across Georgia Strait from their farm. The Indians would either cross the Strait to dig up the potatoes themselves, or intercept Bennett as he took his produce by boat to New Westminster. Although these incidents terrorized the young family from Newcastle, England, no physical harm occurred to them.[42]

Despite the fact that Indians outnumbered white settlers by a large margin in the Gulf Islands — the *Colonist* estimated the Cowichan Indians numbered 3,000 in May 1863 — they never attempted to take advantage of their strength and annihilate the intruders.[43] Lack of harmony among the diverse tribes may be one reason why white settlement was achieved without a great deal of violence, but James Douglas' policy of dealing promptly with misdemeanors through the use of Royal Navy gunboats, public trials and hangings must also be credited. Indians up and down the Coast came to fear and respect "King George's men." Because the gunboats were stationed at Esquimalt they were frequently in evidence for the southern coastal tribes as the ships passed among the Islands en route to the Fraser River or further north.[44] By 1885 a correspondent to the *Colonist* could sanguinely report on the Plumper Pass community, "Our Indian Reserve is at present in the hands of a few steady, industrious redmen who are of great use to us in supplying a deeply felt want, to wit, labour at a reasonable price."[45]

Indian-white conflicts involving Plumper Pass settlers were relatively few in number compared to other areas of British Columbia then being settled. Unfortunately, the white residents of the Pass region could not know this at the time. They could only rely on personal courage, their neighbours and the Royal Navy for support.[46]

* * * * *

During the next decade an international cross-section of young men, many with families, commenced homesteading in the Plumper Pass area. Most of these settlers remained permanently, thus providing an egalitarian foundation for the agrarian community. Fear of the Indians did not deter Alexander Nicholson, H. Lee, William Crooks, Nicholas Cook and Hugh Hamilton from establishing pre-emptions on Mayne Island by 1865. By the same date a group of Portuguese fishermen, Juan Bronar, Jose Silvia and Jose F. Silvia, had pre-empted 100 acres for a fishing station on the Galiano side of Plumper Pass, and Theodore Trage and John O'Brien chose to establish farms there.[47]

As the Cariboo gold rush ran its course and the perceived danger from the Indians receded, men hardened by the harsh realities of Barkerville, Keithley Creek and Quesnel Forks were ready to settle down and raise their families in a more favorable climate within British territory. There was likely a "grapevine" in operation because the next wave of settlers knew one another in the north. Jacob Heck, of Prussian origin, and countryman John Puetz had originally registered a pre-emption together at Swamp Creek in the Cariboo in 1861. Heck had subsequently operated a ferry near Keithley Creek while Puetz had worked as a labourer for various mining operations. On May 20, 1870, they registered claims on adjoining parcels of land, 120 acres each, on Mayne Island. Heck's pre-emption partially included the abandoned claims of Greavy and Mayers.[48]

Although Henry "Scotty" Georgeson did not register his pre-emption until 1873, we know from details of the Robert Clarke murder that he was living on Galiano in 1870. Georgeson had come to Victoria from the Shetland Islands in the 1850's, and had owned a stopping house at Beaver Pass, Lightning Creek, near Barkerville, in 1862.[49]

Next to arrive were William T. (Tom) Collinson, his wife Mary, and two children in 1871. He had met Heck in the Cariboo and had settled at Sumas Prairie in 1863, before

The first lighthouse keeper on Mayne Island, Henry "Scotty" Georgeson with wife Sophie and grandchild. Mary Ellen Georgeson photo.

The original lighthouse at Georgina Point, Mayne Island, with fog station at left, background. Jack Aitken photo.

abandoning his claim in favor of Mayne Island. Under the Land Ordinance of 1870, Collinson was able to pre-empt 160 acres. He was joined in 1871 by Fred Robson, supposedly a partner, who pre-empted 160 acres bordering the Collinson claim.[50]

The one new family on Mayne Island without a gold rush background were John and Louisa Silva. John arrived from the Azores in the late 1860's and operated a grocery store in Victoria for several years before marrying Louisa, a Cowichan Indian, and moving to Village Bay in 1873.[51]

In August 1874 the provincial government assigned George Turner, formerly of the Royal Engineers, to survey Mayne Island. (see map p. 11) A notice in the *British Columbia Gazette,* November 27, 1875, announced that all vacant Crown Land on Mayne Island was open for pre-emption with the exception of twenty parcels that had already been claimed. Five years later the *Gazette* listed only thirty-six parcels remaining.[52] Once the legal survey was completed, the settlers could register their claims properly and pay for them outright if the necessary $2.50 worth of improvements per acre had been carried out. Pre-emptions had been recognized prior to government survey if a written request had been made to the Land Commissioner and a $2.00 fee paid.[53] This method of registration carried with it an element of risk. William Collinson lost the first of his two pre-emptions on Sumas Prairie when it was claimed as part of an Indian reserve.[54]

The first settlers on Mayne Island had required a strong sense of self-reliance to secure their land and establish their farms in a semi-isolated marine environment. During the ensuing years they would have to work together to obtain vital community services such as the post office and police protection, in order that their personal investments would prove worthwhile.

MAP No. 2

The Original Provincial Government Survey Map, Prepared by George Turner in 1874 (Surveys and Lands Records Branch, Ministry of Lands, Parks and Housing, with permission)

Tom Collinson and the Miners Bay wharf built in 1885. ca. 1900. Photo courtesy Margaret Bennett.

Tom Collinson's residence (the first post office) and sloop at Miners Bay. Jack Aitken photo.

2

THE PLUMPER PASS COMMUNITY: 1875-1900

During the next quarter century the frontier settlement at Plumper Pass evolved into the social center of the outer Gulf Islands. Miners Bay, on the steamer route between Victoria and New Westminster, became the focal point of efforts to provide various services to the rising community. Eventually, the wharf, post office, stores, church, community hall, and police lockup would be located here. In addition, Mayne Island experienced the first demands for natural resources from the growing population and industries on the mainland. By 1900 the island was supplying fuel for the Fraser River canneries, and vacation facilities for the middle class of Vancouver and New Westminster.

The provincial government built the first wharf in the outer Gulf Islands at Miners Bay in 1878. This facility permitted the shipment of farm produce by steamer, thus enabling local farms to develop on a larger scale. The wharf also provided settlers on Mayne Island with a strong claim for a post office when regular mail delivery became a possibility.[1]

Both the implementation of postal service for the outer Gulf Islands and the duties it entailed were fraught with difficulties. Initially, residents had rowed out and intercepted the Hudson's Bay Company steamer when they wished to dispatch mail, or paid someone 50¢ to $1.00 to do the chore for them. Attended by rumours that the provincial government planned to build a wharf at Miners Bay in the near future, they submitted a petition for postal service to Ottawa in 1876. (Salt Spring had been granted a government mail service in 1874.) The unsuccessful petition was submitted on behalf of all the residents of Plumper Pass, but the nine signatures it contained were from Mayne Island only. A second petition, submitted in 1879, contained nineteen signatures from residents of Mayne, Saturna, North Pender and Galiano Islands. Although the Postmaster General approved this request, a delay ensued while a replacement was found for Isaac Tod, the man initially proposed for postmaster. William Collinson, who operated a small trading enterprise, finally accepted the position in 1880, and postal service commenced November 1st of that year. A mail slot was inserted into the side of Collinson's house, located near the new wharf. This post office served all the outer Gulf Islands: Saturna, Tumbo, Samuel, North and South Pender, Prevost,

The R. P. Rithet *served the Gulf Islands in the summertime, only. Marine regulations prohibited stern wheelers from crossing Georgia Strait in winter. PABC photo 23753.*

Galiano and Mayne. The steamers delivered mail two or three times a week, which gave outer Islands residents an excellent excuse to take time off from their homesteading chores and row to Mayne Island for a visit and groceries.[2]

Collinson received $50 per year for his postal duties. This money was well-earned for he frequently had to row out to the steamer while the ship hove to in Miners Bay, to transfer mail, passengers and freight. Because of the strong tides in the Pass (up to seven or eight knots), the steamer captains were reluctant to use the Miners Bay wharf after dark, especially at 2 a.m. when Tom had to meet a weekly Victoria to Vancouver mail train sailing.[3] The transfer of baggage and bodies in close proximity to the dangerous sidewheels of the *Yosemite* and *Princess Louise,* and the sternwheel of the *R. P. Rithet,* was a difficult feat. Emma Higgs of South Pender remembered huge hands reaching up to her in the darkness as she and her young son climbed down the ship's ladder to Collinson's waiting rowboat, on their arrival from England in 1893. One Mayne Island woman and her baby were drowned a year earlier when the sternwheel of the *R. P. Rithet* swamped their rowboat.[4]

No doubt a major asset to the settlers was the fact that William Smithe, MLA for Cowichan and the Islands, had been Minister of Finance and Agriculture from August 10, 1876, to June 1878, and was Premier and Minister of Lands and Works from January 29, 1883, until March 28, 1887. Following complaints from Gulf Islands farmers, the legislature passed the Sheep Run Protection Act in 1877, that prevented farmers on the San Juan Islands and elsewhere in Washington Territory from placing their sheep out to pasture on any of the Gulf Islands as far north as Lighthouse Island (at Nanaimo).

During the years that Smithe served in government office, Mayne Island acquired the post office, wharf, school and lighthouse, and work began on roads to link all these services together. Duplication of services on the other Gulf Islands proceeded more slowly, thus reinforcing Mayne's social importance. Following a petition for a school in 1880, the provincial government awarded a $200 building contract to local resident William Robson. Classes commenced in October 1883 with teacher Mrs. Annie Monk,

*Mrs. Annie Monk, Mayne Island's first
schoolteacher in 1883. Photo courtesy W.
R. C. Patrick.*

*James Sinclair taught school on Mayne
Island from 1893 to 1902. Photo courtesy
Dorothy Somers.*

and an enrollment of thirty children from Galiano and Saturna, as well as Mayne.
Smithe made a point to attend final exercises in June 1884, and again in 1885, handing
out prizes and urging the parents to support good education.[5]

With Captain John Irving at the helm, Smithe arrived on board the *Princess Louise*
December 4, 1885, to open officially a new provincial government wharf, built as a
replacement for the 1878 structure. This new dock was twice as wide as the first wharf,
and jutted almost 50 feet farther into Miners Bay to receive the sidewheelers. Captain
Irving pronounced it "the best on either the New Westminster or Nanaimo routes."[6]

The opening celebrations for the wharf revealed two intriguing sides to the Plumper
Pass community. More than 150 people attended from Mayne and the other islands.
The lighthouse tender *Sir James Douglas,* which had visited Mayne Island frequently
while the lighthouse was being built at Georgina Point, lent flags for decorating the
wharf, a group of schoolboys fired a welcoming volley from rifles, and John Puetz
arranged for a "cold collation" to be served at his new hotel and store, recently erected
nearby. In spite of the festivities and merriment the islanders, nonetheless, took the
opportunity to present a list of grievances to Captain Irving regarding passenger
services.[7] This list is the first record of dissatisfaction with steamship service that, in
time, became a chronic complaint. To the islanders, adequate water transportation
went hand in hand with progress.

* * * * *

As the residents of Plumper Pass watched black clouds of smoke rising over the
burning city of Vancouver on Sunday, June 13, 1886, they could look with considerable

The oldest photograph available of a Mayne Island class was taken ca. 1892 by Hannah Maynard of Victoria. (l to r) Eliza Robson, Nellie Patterson, Alice Heck, Bob Harris, Andy Deacon, Lily Jack, Annie Robson, Mrs. Elsie Patterson, teacher. Seated: David Bennett, Green Patterson, Stanley Robson, Fred Bennett, Ethel Harris, Elsie Patterson and Gertie Jack. Photo courtesy Vera Greene.

relief at their own situation where, thanks to hard work, their farms were increasing in productivity and providing more than an adequate living. Surplus produce was taken to the mainland or Vancouver Island on a regular basis. The inauguration of the Victoria and Sidney Railway six years later, in 1894, made Victoria the preferred destination for many Islands farmers.[8]

A report to the Department of Agriculture by local resident W. H. Mawdsley, in 1893, listed the produce and livestock raised on Jacob Heck's farm. Rather than concentrating on one or two types of livestock or produce, mixed farming provided the best returns. Spring wheat, oats, peas and hay were harvested, as well as potatoes, mangolds, carrots, turnips and onions. In addition to these crops, Heck raised chickens, receiving 30¢ a dozen for eggs. He claimed that the market was always good for poultry. Sheep raising, which provided much of the income for farmers on Pender and Saturna, was not as popular on Mayne because of the larger proportion of productive land. Berkshire pigs and shorthorn cattle were raised for meat, and Jersey cows for milk.[9]

Most farmers had planted substantial fruit orchards and these matured in the early 1890's. The young trees were not grown from seed brought from England in a midshipman's pocket — an item of folklore borrowed from the history of Fort Vancouver — but were purchased from local nurseries and from distant points such as Walla Walla, Washington, and St. Thomas, Ontario. One new resident, T. R. Figg, imported his trees from England. In 1890, Figg represented Mayne Island for the Apple Growers Association, and Thomas Bennett, Jacob Heck and Tom Collinson were members of the Islands Agricultural and Fruit Growers Association, which included fruit growers on all the Gulf Islands. Fruit from island farms sold well in the cities until Okanagan produce took over the market in the early 1900's.[10]

Dairy farmers and sheep ranchers in the Gulf Islands were members of the Dairymen's Association and Flockmasters. They joined with the other Islands farmers to exhibit animals and produce in the large fairs at New Westminster and Victoria every fall, never failing to win prizes.

The most successful Plumper Pass farmers with large acreages took advantage of local government tenders to earn additional money working on new roads, or public buildings such as the lighthouse and school. In addition, Tom Collinson, John Puetz and William Robson held various local government offices of postmaster, tax collector and Justice of the Peace, and they were also store/hotel proprietors. Subsistence farmers such as Charles Groth had to be even more ingenious to earn an adequate living.[11]

As a young immigrant from Schlesweig-Holstein, Charles kept a diary for the first six years that he homesteaded on Galiano, 1881 to 1887, and from his careful entries we can gain an understanding of an immigrant's new life, one hundred years ago. He moved to Galiano Island in 1879 after working for Noah Buckley (Buckly) on North Pender Island, where he learned the rudiments of farming. By 1881 he had married sixteen-year-old Elizabeth Georgeson, daughter of Sophie and Henry, and registered his pre-emption of 160 acres. Until Charles could establish a productive farm, he raised sheep in partnership with a neighbour, John (possibly John O'Brien). Despite heavy

18

Charles and Elizabeth Groth, Galiano, with children (l to r) Charles, John, Katharine, William and Frederick. Provincial Archives of B. C. photo 42256.

losses to cougars, they managed to round up a flock of lambs each fall and take them by sloop to market in New Westminster. Charles bought lumber for a barn at New Westminster with the money from the second year's crop of lambs, then stopped at Ladner for a cow before returning across Georgia Strait. The young family apparently resided with Henry Georgeson until they could move into their new home in December 1882.[12]

By making use of abundant natural resources, bartering with neighbours on Galiano and Mayne, and selling produce in Victoria, Nanaimo and New Westminster, Charles was able to maintain a comfortable living for his family. Deer skins and ducks were sold to Chinese merchants in Victoria; oil rendered from dogfish livers sold at New Westminster for 25¢ a gallon as grease for logging skids. Deer, grouse and ducks provided free meat year round for the price of ammunition, and salmon and cod were salted or smoked and dried for the winter. Charles traded calves for potatoes and wheat from Jacob Heck's established farm, and bought other supplies from Collinson, Puetz and Robson. In addition, his sheep shearing skills brought remuneration annually.[13]

Groth's father-in-law, Henry Georgeson, fished for Alexander Ewen's cannery on the Fraser River, and served on the Sandheads light station before he became the first lighthouse keeper at Georgina Point, Mayne Island, in June 1885.[14] Groth's diary records that Charles also fished on the Fraser River in the 1880's. Salmon runs for the years 1881 to 1883 were excellent. In 1882 Charles and his partners caught 6,901 salmon, which sold for four cents each. The year 1886 had a poor salmon run. Charles felt he was "not making salt" and did not want to fish again.[15] Public works projects supplied further income. Charles worked building the Georgina Point lighthouse in 1884, and won a contract to build 725 yards of road on Galiano in 1885 for $175.00.[16]

While still a relative stranger in a new land, Charles took part in the affairs of the community. He willingly rowed across Active Pass to attend several preliminary school meetings before the first school in the district was erected on Mayne Island in 1883, and he registered his vote during an election in 1885. When Galiano residents acquired their own school in 1892, Charles served as a trustee.[17] Although his farming efforts, as described in his diary, were less productive than the large farms of Jacob Heck and Fred Robson, Charles Groth can be considered typical of many immigrants who came to British Columbia before 1900. He quietly made his contribution to the rural history of the province by working hard, and living in harmony with friends, neighbours and the environment.

* * * * *

Despite their isolation, both small and large farms in the Plumper Pass area were vulnerable to smugglers and cattle rustlers. The settlers soon demanded effective police protection. As early as 1867 James Greavy complained that his ranch stock on Mayne Island had not increased because of rustlers, but by 1890 a petty annoyance had reached epidemic proportions. Home base for the thieves appeared to be in the San Juan Islands. The many protected bays to the south and east in the Gulf Islands, such as

Fiddler's Cove, Saturna, provided ideal locations for their clandestine operations. The wharf, postal service and central location at Miners Bay were important considerations when Superintendent of Provincial Police F. S. Hussey had to choose an Islands headquarters for a special constable.[18]

Following numerous appeals to Hussey by the Gulf Islands farmers, Constable Thomas M. Robb was eventually assigned to Gulf Islands patrol in March 1893. He boarded at Mayne Island House, operated by William Robson, J.P., at Miners Bay. Robb was replaced by William McNeill in September 1893, and in May 1894 Arthur Drummond was appointed on a permanent basis, followed by Stephen Hoskins in 1898 and Angus Ego in 1900. A police launch from Victoria assisted the constables in patrolling the Islands during the summers of 1893 and 1894.[19]

For all other seasons of the year, and from 1895 onwards, the only method of transportation for the constables was a sixteen-foot rowboat equipped with a sail. Efforts by Arthur Drummond to secure a steam-powered launch in 1897 proved futile.[20] Officially termed "Plumper Pass and the Islands," the district extended from the United States-Canadian border to Porlier Pass at the north end of Galiano Island, and from the Georgia Strait west to Vancouver Island. The more densely populated Salt Spring Island was thus a responsibility, and from 1900 to 1905 parts of North Saanich were also included. Frequently, travelling in the line of duty did not stop at these boundaries. Stephen Hoskins recalls having to walk from Cowichan Bay to Duncan in order to contact other district constables, and all serious cases had to be tried in Victoria or New Westminster. When investigating the theft of a boat in October 1894, Drummond journeyed as far as Seattle, rowing to Waldron Island where he then caught the steamer. Other boat thefts involved trips to the canneries at Ladner on the Fraser River or to the growing city of Vancouver.[21]

Besides smuggling, cattle rustling and boat thefts, the constables had to investigate pit-lamping and the illegal sale of liquor to the Indians, deliver trading and liquor licences approved by the Superintendent of Police, and report any outbreak of communicable diseases. Constable Ego vaccinated thirty-eight people on Galiano for smallpox in 1903. Cannery season on the Fraser River caused a mass migration of workers through Active Pass, with subsequent thefts and breaking and entering. The constable on duty remained at Mayne Island while water traffic was heavy during June and September.[22]

There were few unusual deaths to investigate. Most were from drowning or natural causes, although timber clearing by the Japanese resulted in the accidental deaths of men on Pender, Galiano and Mayne.[23] Constable Ego displayed incredible zeal when he dealt with the most sensational case of the period, the shooting death of recluse Barnard (also known as Marnard) Wenzel on Tumbo Island in 1903. When the Vancouver *Daily Province* suggested that the wheels of justice turned slowly in the Gulf Islands, William Collinson, now a Justice of the Peace, came to Ego's defense:

> I notice in your issue of the *Daily Province* of the 24th inst. an article reflecting very unjustly on Constable Ego re. the slaying of Marnard Wenzel, better known as Jack the Ripper. Let me give you the facts as far as affects Constable Ego. At 12

Bound for the Fraser River the steam tug Squid *passes through Active Pass, towing a fleet of Indian fishing boats and canoes from the west coast of Vancouver Island ca. 1905. Jack Aitken photo.*

a.m. on the 14th inst. Captain Shultz appeared before me asking for a warrant against a man supposed to be Jack the Ripper — for shooting at him in the twilight of the evening of the 12th inst. telling me that he had fired a shot back at Wenzel as he (Wenzel) was preparing for another shot, and he was afraid that he might have wounded Wenzel, and urged that the constable make what haste he could to the scene of the tragedy.

I made out the warrant and handed it to Constable Ego, and although [it was] blowing strongly at the time, Ego left immediately in the sixteen-foot rowboat for Tumbo Island, twelve miles along the open Gulf, and in less than three hours had found Wenzel dead. By 10 o'clock that night Ego arrived here at the Pass with Captain Shultz, whom he had picked up on the way. Two o'clock next morning found Ego on his way to Salt Spring Island, ten miles distant, to notify the Coronor. Having fulfilled his mission he landed back at the Pass in the afternoon, at once setting to work to empanel a jury, and by next morning had everything ready, jury, gravedigger and a coffin to boot — making the latter himself. All this forty-four miles was performed in a rowboat, right down steady rowing; and you say Ego travels by slow freight. All the same, if you have a swifter man on your staff let us hear of him and he shall be dubbed The Imperial Limited.[24]

All three of the permanent constables were outstanding examples of dedication and hard work. They were shrewd judges of character, quickly learning to separate local feuds from legitimate complaints. With a salary of only $60-$65 per month, they were often out of pocket for travelling expenses until reimbursed. Nevertheless, they accepted their responsibilities without complaint and easily gained the respect of the

The Plumper Pass lockup built in December 1896, and now operated as a museum by the Mayne Island Agricultural Society.

Stephen Hoskins, Provincial Police constable, Mayne Island, from 1898 to 1900. Photo courtesy Clive Hoskins.

Islands residents. "As a policeman, you looked upon any place you hung your hat as home," Stephen Hoskins recalled. "Everyone made you welcome. I always had blankets in the boat, and a certain amount of grub. Sometimes you'd strike a poor shack, pull in, take the best they had, and give 'em what you had of yours."[25]

Weather permitting, regular patrols were made of all the Islands, but the Superintendent ocasionally heard from a resident who felt he had been neglected. To one complaint raised by H. L. Robertson of Moresby Island, Drummond provided a lengthy description of his rowboat patrols for a five month period, from January to May 1896. Moresby was a small island, with only one farm, but Drummond had checked its shores for smugglers at least once every two weeks during that time.[26]

Despite the vigilance of the constables, smugglers did persist in making their visits, albeit with less frequency. One crafty fellow by the name of Old Burke became something of a folk hero on South Pender, where for a number of years he made cautious visits, exchanging chickens, tobacco or whatever the residents would accept for sheep's wool. When the United States Customs authorities discovered a large amount of wool coming from one small, rocky island in the San Juan group, they laid a trap and Old Burke's smuggling days came to an end.[27]

Seldom did the constables take time off from work. Before doing so, the Superintendent had to be notified and a temporary replacement found. Drummond made full use of his free time by organizing camping parties for his friends on Saturna and South Pender. On one occasion he brought his flotilla to Miners Bay for salmon fishing.[28]

With regard to the personal history of the constables, little is known about the two temporary constables, McNeill and Robb, except that they had been stationed earlier in Victoria. Robb was subsequently transferred to Ashcroft where his health broke down, as a consequence of having been "sandbagged" by some prisoners at Mayne.[29]

Arthur Drummond and Stephen Hoskins had lived in the Gulf Islands for several years before being appointed. Drummond was one of three brothers who resided on Saturna, scions of Drummond castle in Scotland. Drummond later served in the Kootenay region as police constable. Stephen Hoskins had left England in 1890, homesteading on the Prairies before coming to British Columbia in 1894. He lived on Galiano for two years and initially turned down the opportunity to join the Provincial Police in 1896: "I told them I would never make a policeman in 1,000 years — I hadn't the guts." After serving as a temporary replacement for Drummond, he finally accepted the permanent position when Drummond was transferred in 1898. Hoskins subsequently served with the Victoria city detachment and later in the Kootenays before becoming a government agent.[30]

It was not until four years of police work had been completed in the Gulf Islands that a lockup was deemed necessary. With a wharf and post offfice, and a central location, Miners Bay was the logical site even though Robson's Bay (Horton Bay) and locations on the other Islands had also been suggested. Arthur Drummond's friend and neighbour on Saturna, Warburton Pike, generously donated property situated two hundred yards up the road from the wharf at Miners Bay, and Levan Cullison, a Galiano resident, was awarded the building contract for $320. The lockup, which was completed in December 1896, measured 15 by 23 feet, and contained two cells and a single front room large enough to hold a magistrate's court, when necessary.[31] Henry Freer, arrested on a charge of larceny, had the dubious honor of being the first prisoner. Freer had been seen wandering around Galiano Island, collecting wild plants for his hair growing and freckle removing preparations, and was suspected of breaking and entering a home at Cowichan Gap (Porlier Pass). Because the lumber had not yet dried on the new lockup, Drummond borrowed blankets and a bed from Robson's hotel so that Freer would not have to sleep on the damp floor. The unfortunate prisoner spent a few miserable days incarcerated before he was found not guilty by local magistrates Robert Grubb and W. H. Mawdsley.[32]

During the months of January and February 1897, Drummond continued to make Robson's hotel his residence. He submitted hotel receipts for room and board until Superintendent Hussey informed him that he would have to consider the new lockup as his home — no further charges for meals or bed would be expected from Mayne. The Department supplied a stove and table and chairs, but the policeman was responsible for his own bed. Not until 1900 did Constable Ego dare to suggest to the Superintendent that the government purchase the bed of the previous constable, Stephen Hoskins.[33]

Precisely how many prisoners stayed in the lockup is not known because monthly police reports for the period in question are unavailable. The existing evidence suggests that the building saw more use as a police residence than as a detention center. Henry Georgeson's diary notes that a local resident was kept overnight in the lockup December 26, 1912, and that the next day in magistrate's court he was sentenced to one month in prison for trespassing. The sentence would have been served in Victoria or on the mainland. It is possible that this was the last recorded detention in the lockup; certainly, the memories of long-time residents tend to corroborate this assumption.[34]

The only other lockup in the Gulf Islands was a building erected in 1886 at Central Settlement on Salt Spring (at the junction of Vesuvius Bay and North End Roads).[35] This site was inconveniently located three miles inland from the Ganges steamer landing. In 1911, six years after headquarters for the Gulf Islands had been transferred to Salt Spring, Constable J. O'Hara wrote a long letter to Colin S. Campbell, Acting Superintendent of Police, requesting that Mayne once again be made the Islands headquarters. He stressed the importance of its central location in the district compared to Salt Spring, and the facts that Mayne Island had the only hotel in the outer Islands and a recently installed telephone office.[36] O'Hara was allowed to have the Mayne lockup refurbished, but it appears that Salt Spring remained the Gulf Islands headquarters from 1905 onwards. One vast improvement to the policemean's lot was his method of transportation. Because all the Islands had wharves and adequate boat service by 1911, the constables were allowed to use steamer transportation to visit the outer Islands, rather than a rowboat.[37]

* * * * *

The spiritual and recreational needs of the emerging community were not overlooked. As early as the 1880's ministers from Victoria and New Westminster began

In August 1900, Ralph Grey of Samuel Island and Canon W. F. L. Paddon transported the 400 lb. sandstone font for St. Mary Magdalene Church by rowboat from East Point Lighthouse, Saturna. Mabel Foster photo.

St. Mary Magdalene Church was consecrated in 1898. Marie Elliott photo.

Canon W. F. L. Paddon, with Mrs. Paddon and daughter Theo. Jack Aitken photo.

making occasional visits for christenings or marriages. Local residents took care of burials on private property or used the cemeteries on the mainland and Vancouver Island, because there was no official cemetery on Mayne Island until 1911. In 1884 Charles Groth recorded in his diary that a Reverend Mr. Woods rowed across Plumper Pass from Mayne Island with Mrs. Margaret Deacon to baptize two of the Groth children.[38] Sunday school also began that year on Mayne Island, but church services were sporadic until 1896 when Canon William Francis Locke Paddon of the Anglican Church commenced regular visits from Victoria. Services were initially conducted in the school or Robson's Hotel.[39] William Collinson volunteered to donate land for a church in 1893, but his offer was not acted upon and, instead, Warburton Pike, donor of the lockup property at Miners Bay, provided the site for the church as well. In 1897 Bishop William W. Perrin allotted a fund, established by Mrs. Baynton Starkey of Great Cheswell, England, for the purchase of a steam launch for an Islands mission, towards the construction of a church. The funds amounted to $836, which Canon Paddon considered sufficient when combined with local pledges. Architect J. C. Keith, designer of Victoria's Christ Church Cathedral, provided plans, and Galiano carpenter William Cain supervised the construction. On Easter Sunday, 1898, the church was consecrated by Right Reverend Perrin, Bishop of Columbia. Representatives from Galiano, Gossip, Mayne, Pender, Saturna and Samuel served on the church board. Paddon journeyed from Victoria fortnightly to hold services until he moved to the island permanently in 1904.[40]

Paddon's close supervision of the construction and furnishing of the church is responsible for the unusual baptismal font, a large block of beach drift sandstone, carved into an attractive shape by wave action. Paddon and Ralph Grey transported the 400 pound rock by rowboat from East Point, Saturna, in 1900, in a laborious operation that took them eighteen hours. Mounted near the door of the church, the

Built ca. 1900, the community hall initially served residents of all the outer Gulf Islands. New Year's Eve dances were a traditional event until the 1950's. With few breaks, the annual Fall Fair has been held at the hall since 1925.

sandstone font reminds all worshippers as they enter of the timeless link between land and sea.[41]

About 1899 — the precise date is uncertain — the first community hall in the outer Islands was erected at Miners Bay, providing a center for dances and parties attended by residents of the Islands for the next fifty years. Thereafter, annual New Year's Eve dances were held at Mayne Island, with more than one hundred merrimakers in attendance from all the Islands. Victoria Day celebrations were another annual, inter-island event that ended in a dance at the hall in the evening. The Maple Leaf Club formed in 1903 to care for the building and, like the church board, contained members from the other Islands.[42]

* * * * *

Despite their isolation from one another, the shared adversity of having to negotiate the dangerous waterways of the Gulf Islands in rowboats provided the residents with a common bond. Until the advent of gas powered motors in the early 1900's, tides and weather controlled the possibility that residents on the other Islands would attend social events at Mayne Island. Winifred Grey of Samuel Island was one of the few Gulf Island women who enjoyed boating (with her husband, Ralph, or sister, Mabel), but she summed up the cautious attitude of her family thus:

Four Mayne Island men prior to departing on a sealing expedition. (l to r) Hunter Jack, Melville Collinson; (seated) Sam Collinson and Joseph Bodine. Bodine drowned off the coast of Japan in 1894. Photo courtesy Margaret Bennett.

Wind and tide played a large part in our lives on the islands. All our comings and goings were ordered by them to a great extent, except in an emergency. Ralph had a tide book issued by the government, which he always consulted before we planned any trip. Mabel and I never sailed alone; the gusts of wind and sudden squalls in those enclosed waters were too treacherous.[43]

The cohesiveness of the small Plumper Pass community was also due to the fact that everyone knew one another's business. This closeness can explain why second generation sons and daughters did not intermarry — they simply knew one another too well — but it also explains why relations among the residents were occasionally discordant. On the positive side, this closeness was a decided advantage when the residents required health care or companions to share in leisure-time adventures.

The island farms could not support all the children of the large pioneer families. Only one or two second generation members chose to remain on the island and help elderly parents with the upkeep of land, buildings and livestock. The sea beckoned many of the young men. At least six left before 1900 for jobs on coastal steamers or on whaling and sealing vessels that travelled as far as Japan. Other seasonal work was found in the canneries on the Fraser River.[44]

Most young women on Mayne Island married without having worked away from home, although two of William Collinson's daughters worked as housekeepers in Victoria — one even going to the Klondike — before marrying. No marriages were contracted between the immediate descendants of the oldest families: Hecks, Robsons, Deacons, Georgesons, Collinsons and Bennetts. There were inter-island marriages, however, and the rest involved new families on Mayne Island or young men and women from the mainland or Victoria.[45]

Many of the early settlers on Mayne Island lived long, healthy lives. A combination of hard, outdoor work, wholesome food and freedom from stress ensured that Elsie and Thomas Bennett, Sophie and Henry Georgeson, Catherine Heck, and Fred Robson reached eighty years or more. Until 1897, when Dr. G. R. Baker became the first resident physician on the Islands at Salt Spring, the settlers took care of their own health requirements.[46] Charles Groth's wife Elizabeth gave birth to seven children before her death from tuberculosis at age 35 in 1899. With the exception of one baby who was born at New Westminster, all the children were probably born at home.[47]

On Mayne Island, Ann Robson and Elsie Bennett were known for their skills in midwifery. Women from the other Islands boarded with them during confinement, but the safe delivery of a healthy baby was always a risk. Elizabeth Grimmer of North Pender gave birth to a son in a rowboat on the way to Elsie Bennett's, and Emma Higgs of South Pender, who also relied on Elsie Bennett, lost four of her babies because of birth complications.[48] Since there would not be a hospital at Salt Spring until 1914, most babies continued to be born at home or at the Robson's or Bennett's homes on Mayne until about 1920. For those few mothers who could afford it, the alternative was to stay in a private nursing home in Victoria or on the mainland.[49]

Indian women like Sophie preferred the attentions of their own native doctors when sick. Henry Georgeson used to fetch Indian Tom from the Helen Point Reserve to care for his wife, but the egalitarian nature of the community allowed Ann Robson to provide nursing care when Sophie was terminally ill.[50]

The happy occasions of births and marriages were occasionally augmented by such light-hearted pastimes as cock fighting and even searching for gold. Cock fighting took place primarily among the English remittance settlers on South Pender and Saturna Islands. An English settler with a hooded game cock under his arm, en route to a neighbour, was a familiar sight on South Pender on a Sunday morning.[51]

Following the Cariboo gold rush, stories of buried gold were part of the folklore of many communities in British Columbia. The homestead of Alex Nicholson, an early Mayne Island settler who had mined in Australia, California and the Cariboo, was the site of an intensive hunt in 1895. An earlier search had been carried out in 1875 upon Nicholson's death when one oldtimer claimed he had caught Alex counting his gold on the table in his cabin, and noticed that a brick had been removed from the fireplace hearth. Nothing was found beneath the bricks except $4.50 in silver coins. A resident's dream, showing where the gold might now be found, led to the 1895 treasure hunt. The community spent two days probing Nicholson's orchard with pointed metal bars but again came away empty-handed. Attempts were still being made to find the legendary cache as late as 1955.[52]

Thomas and Alice Bennett, ca. 1915. Photo courtesy Margaret Bennett.

Fred Robson, shown here at age 80, established a homestead adjacent to Tom Collinson in 1871. Mabel Foster photo.

In 1898 the Klondike gold rush beckoned Ralph Grey of Samuel, Gerald Payne of Saturna, Edward Winstanley of Galiano and Fred Robson of Mayne Island. PABC photo 61848

Excitement generated by the Klondike gold rush was hard to ignore. Despite the large number of merchants in Vancouver by 1898, Victoria was also an important supply depot. Residents of the Pass area were treated almost daily to the spectacle of passing ships, heavily laden with men, supplies and barking dogs. Edward Winstanley of Galiano and Fred Robson of Mayne, joined Gerald Payne, Saturna and Ralph Grey, Samuel, in one venture to the north. Winstanley made several more trips, but it would seem the others were more curious than ambitious.[53]

* * * * *

The small community, semi-isolated by water, experienced a build-up of tension from time to time, which was often released by using a public servant as a target. The tribulations of feisty William Tom Collinson are a good example.

When Collinson attempted to secure the position of police constable at Sumas Prairie in 1867, Chartres Brew described him as "notorious for not speaking the truth. Winifred Grey had this to say after meeting Tom on a visit to Miners Bay in 1897:

Tall, lean Mr. Collinson was the postmaster, and held the record for having the largest feet; and being the island's champion liar — or shall we say, Romantic. No matter what the topic of conversation, he could lie, and lie interestingly — as long as anyone would listen — about his experiences and utterly impossible exploits in that particular line, with a perfectly straight face; and then tell the same episode next time, with varying circumstances. It was a real gift.[54]

Thomas Figg, a newcomer to Mayne Island in 1884, described Tom as the "connecting link with the outside world, careful over his postal duties and always willing to receive or impart gossip from or to the outside world as he ferries his passengers to the *Yosemite* or *Teaser.*" Tom thus held a precarious position in the community. He had received about five years of schooling in North Yorkshire before emigrating with his family to Gray County, Canada West, in 1850, and this education put him in good stead when a postmaster was sought. Tom's name does not appear on the petition for the post office in 1876; omission may be explained by some local animosity or by absenteeism.[55]

Tom had been instrumental in arranging for a school on Mayne Island in 1883, yet when he was being considered for the Justice of the Peace position that same year a petition was sent to Premier Smithe requesting that he not be appointed.[56] Once he took over the postal operation in 1880 and became a public servant, Tom was a constant target for complaints. Fortunately, he was every bit a match for his detractors.

In 1886 Washington Grimmer, Justice of the Peace for North Pender Island, prepared a petition bearing sixteen signatures to the postal authorities, claiming that Tom was opening residents' letters and broadcasting the contents. The chief postal inspector from Victoria, E. F. Fletcher, carried out an investigation, taking affidavits from six of the petitioners. Fletcher concluded that Tom may have been "incautious" in speaking about handwritten addresses on the envelopes, but that transactions at the Plumper Pass post office were being carried out in the proper manner: "The prejudice existing against him appears to be strengthened from the fact that he is a trader, in a small way, in opposition to the store kept by Mr. John Puetz, who with his friends, seems to be the chief mover in the complaints brought against him." Tom was to get his revenge a few years later when he led a petition against a liquor licence that William Robson, Puetz's friend, wanted for his Mayne Island Hotel.[57]

Perhaps Toms's most difficult fight occured in 1894 when John W. Rudd attempted to claim part of the Collinson pre-emption at Miners Bay, stating that Tom had not carried out the necessary amount of improvements on the property to entitle him legally to hold onto it. Fourteen pages of letters and petitions are bound into the British Columbia *Sessional Papers* for 1897, covering the charges and counter-charges between the two parties and their island supporters. Tom won out in the end, but at considerable cost in time and money. Surveyors had to be paid and witnesses secured for petitions and documents.[58]

Tom's role in the community reached a zenith when he was finally made Justice of the Peace in 1897, a position previously held by Puetz and Robson. By this time a larger community, with a resident constable, required more judicial services from Tom than it had from predecessors. Respect for his position and age seems to have tempered any further animosities.[59]

* * * * *

As the community on Mayne Island grew, so also did the urban and industrial demands upon it from the lower mainland. Middle class families from Vancouver and

The Mayne Island Hotel evolved from a small store and boarding house in 1890 to a large hotel complex by 1915. The two-storey addition on the right was demolished but the small house in the middle remained until the hotel burned down in 1923. Photos courtesy Vera Greene, Margaret Bennett, Jesse Steves and Jack Aitken.

New Westminster sought moderately priced summer vacation facilities close to the cities while, at the same time, the salmon canning industry on the Fraser River directly affected the community.

As early at 1883 Plumper Pass had been a desirable destination for one day picnic outings for the Oddfellows fraternity and their families. On August 16 of that year the *Yosemite* from Victoria, *Wilson G. Hunt* from Nanaimo and *R. G. Dunsmuir* from New Westminster brought seven hundred people and a complement of brass bands to the Miners Bay area. Mayne Island's accessibility, combined with such desirable recreational facilities as salmon fishing and sea bathing, caused it to become one of the first resort areas on the north Pacific Coast. By 1900 two hotels and two guest homes were attracting a large number of summer visitors.[60]

John Puetz's small hotel and store, built at Miners Bay about 1885, was enlarged by the next owners, John and Ann Robson, by 1895 to accommodate more guests. In 1892 W. H. Mawdsley formed a company to build a thirty-bedroom hotel on his attractive property near the lighthouse at Georgina Point. Workmen completed the building by September 1893, at a cost in excess of $15,000. Designed by the Victoria architectural firm of Soule and Day to emulate an old English inn, and set in 132 acres of natural landscaping, which also included tennis courts and a cricket green, the elegant, three-storied building was a landmark on Active Pass until it was dismantled in 1958.[61]

Unfortunately, Mawdsley experienced financial difficulties and the hotel was not operated successfully until Warburton Pike foreclosed on a $2500 mortgage in 1895. Between 1896 and 1900, under the genial proprietorship of the Thomas Bennett family and others, the Point Comfort hotel catered to daily and weekly guests, and to picnic outings, with "fresh fruit in season" and "choice wines, spirits and cigars at the bar." The steamers made special stops at the hotel's private wharf to disembark guests. Undoubtedly, the most popular feature at the turn of the century was the hotel's well-stocked bar. Residents of Galiano would risk foul weather and strong tides to enjoy their liquid refreshments on the other side of the Pass. Robson's hotel also had a liquor license, and because there were no other saloons in the outer Gulf Islands, Mayne acquired the nickname "'little Hell." Two petitions were unsuccessful in closing Robson's saloon before 1900. Mayne's dubious popularity continued until Prohibition, but the vote for prohibition in the outer Gulf Islands received positive support only from Pender Island.[62]

With the departure of their eldest children to seek work in Victoria or on the mainland, two other large families on Mayne Island turned their homes into summer boarding houses. Tom Collinson's large home at the head of the government wharf offered rooms for lodgers by 1895,[63] and John and Margaret Deacon were catering to summer visitors by 1891. Five years later they advertised in the New Westminster *Columbian* that their resort was near Plumper Pass and that the steamer would make a special stop at Village Bay, which was

> . . . fortunate in possessing exceptionally fine beaches for bathing, while on the bay boating is practically free from the dangers of tide riffles and storms. In the vicinity, also, are fine mineral springs, containing valuable curative properties.[64]

The Point Comfort Hotel, ca. 1905, with William H. Mawdsley's house and boathouse in the foreground. Jack Aitken photo.

Tom Collinson's residence and boarding house, ca. 1895. H. Maynard photograph.

Little boys who dared to tease Margaret Deacon, were apt to feel the sting of her buggy whip. Photo courtesy Caroline Hopton.

John and Margaret Deacon's boarding house at Village Bay. Photo courtesy Caroline Hopton.

John and Margaret Deacon, Village Bay, with their grandchildren. Photo courtesy Caroline Hopton.

Guests were allowed to roam over the large acreage of the Deacon farm, riding horses or hiking to the top of nearby 700 foot Mount Parke. On mail days they would make the one mile trek to "the Pass" in a horse-drawn wagon. The mineral spring was man-made in 1890 while drill testing for coal. A more favorable result was obtained at Tumbo Island, but the abandoned drill hole, with its wooden shaft, now spilled out sulphur water.[65]

Coincidentally, while Mayne Island experienced an influx of tourists during the summer time, Japanese labourers began arriving as a direct result of the Fraser River canneries. The canneries required not only fish, but large supplies of cordwood for furnaces and charcoal to heat the soldering irons that sealed the cans.[66] Japanese labourers were soon working on all the islands, cutting wood and making charcoal in large, rock walled pits. The fuel supplies would then be shipped by schooner to the Fraser River. When the Tumbo Coal Mining Company was forced to abandon its mining venture because of serious water infiltration, the Japanese miners also turned to wood cutting on Saturna and the other islands.[67] In February 1901 an immigration officer estimated that there were several hundred Japanese cutting wood on Mayne, Pender, Prevost and Galiano, with eighty men on Mayne.[68] The woodcutters were followed by Japanese fishermen who established themselves at St. John's Point on Mayne Island. Local farmers began hiring these men to clear land, and were willing to rent or sell acreage to them. Thus, by 1900 the nucleus of a permanent Japanese community had been formed, and by 1942 it comprised one-third of the entire population of the island. The only other large Japanese community in the Gulf Islands was at Salt Spring.[69]

Unlike North and South Pender Islands, which were proud of their Scottish and English enclaves,[70] Mayne, Salt Spring and Galiano Islands maintained an egalitarian nature until the twentieth century. Germans, Scots, Irish, Portuguese and English, some with Indian wives, did not take time to worry about class distinctions as they struggled to establish their farms. The arrival of the Japanese residents in the late 1890's was accepted as a matter of course, just as their children would be later welcomed at the local school, in sharp contrast to Vancouver and Victoria where Orientals were treated with considerable prejudice.[71]

By 1900 the community on Mayne Island was thriving and its residents confident and optimistic. The first subdivisions had been introduced at Georgina Point and Miners Bay, and the non-Indian population had grown from two men in 1861 to about one hundred men, women and children. They had every right to join with most Canadians as the nation looked forward with anticipation to even greater prosperity and happiness in the new century.[72]

38

MAP No. 3

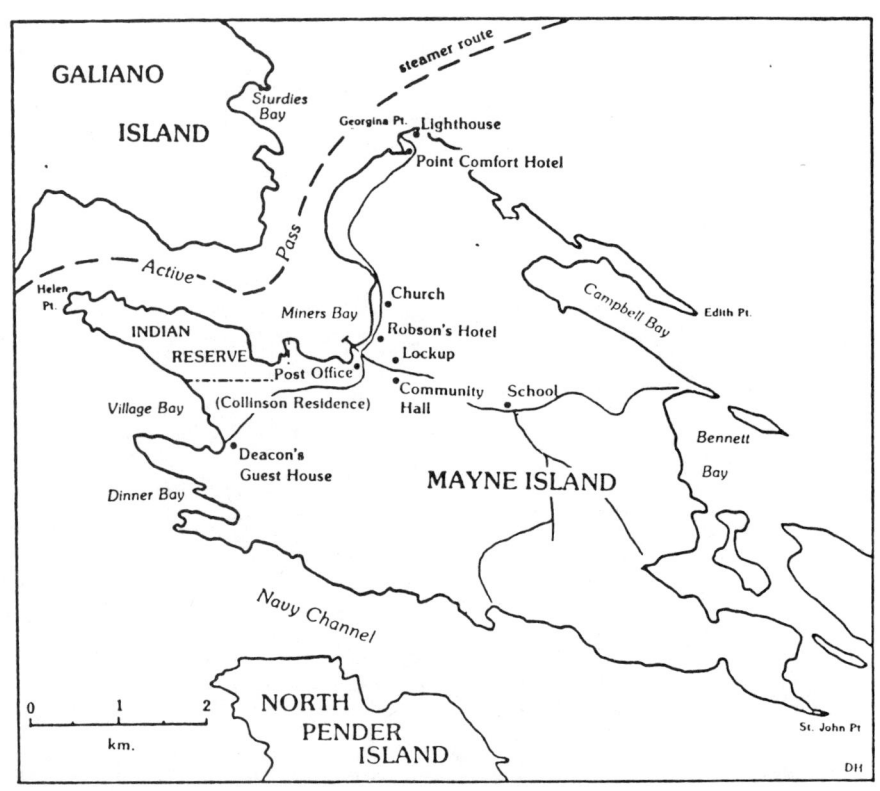

GALIANO

ISLAND

steamer route

Sturdies Bay

Georgina Pt. Lighthouse

Point Comfort Hotel

Pass

Active

Helen Pt.

Miners Bay

Church

Campbell Bay

Edith Pt.

INDIAN
RESERVE

Robson's Hotel

Lockup

Post Office

Community Hall

School

Village Bay

(Collinson Residence)

Deacon's
Guest House

MAYNE ISLAND

Bennett Bay

Dinner Bay

Navy Channel

0   1   2
km.

NORTH
PENDER
ISLAND

St. John Pt

DH

Public Facilities on Mayne Island by 1900

3

COMPLACENCY THEN CONTENTION: 1900-1950

During the next fifty years, local, national and international events challenged the optimism and enthusiasm with which the residents of Mayne Island faced the coming of the twentieth century. The community gradually set aside notions of prosperity and growth in favor of merely enjoying life in a pleasant environment, as they maintained their quiet backwater through two world wars and a depression. The island existed comfortably with the demands of the mainland for vacation facilities, while British pensioned families arrived and the established occidental and Japanese farmers continued to provide the economic base for the community.

Lacking the resources for economic growth, but enjoying low taxes and adequate transportation, the occidental residents of Mayne Island would not have to make many changes to their way of life until the 1950's. Unfortunately, the Japanese residents of the community would experience a complete upheaval in 1942.

As always, the marine environment dominated life in the Gulf Islands. Social activities continued to focus around the arrival of the mail and passenger steamers three or four times a week. The Islands had enjoyed an adequate service from a great variety of vessels, beginning in the 1880's with the sturdy Hudson's Bay sidewheelers *Enterprise* and *Princess Louise,* and followed by *R. P. Rithet, Yosemite, Islander, Teaser (Rainbow), Tees, Otter* and *Charmer* when the Company amalgamated with Canadian Pacific Navigation Company in 1883.[1] The Canadian Pacific Railway Company acquired control of the CPN fleet in 1901, using many of these ships and adding replacements as the older ones were retired. Through the years, captains and crews won the admiration and friendship of many Island residents. A favorite captain would be recognized, even before his ship docked, by the manner in which he blew the three short and one long docking signal on the ship's whistle.[2]

At times, steamship service was also supplied by smaller companies, such as the Victoria Terminal Railway and Ferry Company, which built the Victoria and Sidney Railway in 1894, shortening considerably the distance by ship for passengers and freight bound for Victoria. The company's S.S. *Iroquois* serviced the Gulf Islands from 1901 to 1911, with round trips every Saturday and Wednesday, connecting with the V&S Railway at Sidney. Farmers shipped cream, garden produce and livestock —

The sturdy little H. B. C. sidewheeler Enterprise *(1862-1885) was the first ship to serve the outer Gulf Islands as she plied between Victoria and New Westminster. This photograph is the only one available of the ship, showing her being abandoned following a collision with the* R. P. Rithet *in 1885, off Cadboro Bay. PABC photo 205*

The magnificent Yosemite *was also a popular ship of the Canadian Pacific Navigation fleet, ca. 1900. Photo courtesy Vera Greene.*

The Charmer *served the Islands between World War I and World War II. Her distinctive whistle could be heard easily on Mayne Island as she made her way through the fog, across Georgia Strait to Active Pass. PABC photo 52766*

The Iroquois *in the canal between North and South Pender. PABC photo 12871*

SS Princess Adelaide *on the rocks at Georgina Point in October 1918. Mary Ellen Georgeson photo.*

The Kenkon Maru *#3 aground on Belle Chain reef in 1916, with the steam tug* Dola *standing by. Jack Aitken photo.*

especially lambs — to city markets. In order to avoid the heavy winter seas encountered off South Pender en route to Saturna, a small isthmus of sand was removed between North and South Pender Islands in 1903, allowing the *Iroquois* to make a safer and faster passage among the islands. Besides her regular stops, she could be flagged down along the way. Moonlight cruises were an added attraction during the summer, especially for residents of Victoria and the Saanich peninsula.[3] With almost personalized service the little vessel was also popular for its bar, which the ship's purser opened upon arrival at any wharf. Thirsty islanders took ready advantage of this travelling liquor store that dispensed spirits for $1.25 a bottle.[4]

Even to the untrained eye, the superstructure of the *Iroquois* was obviously top-heavy, and the crew were not always prudent in limiting passenger loads. Mrs. Muriel Page remembers the July 1st holiday excursion to Ganges in 1901 that was squelched by her mother, Mrs. Alfred Cayzer, who noticed (while kneading bread by the kitchen window) that the *Iroquois* was already overloaded with passengers as it approached the Mayne Island dock. With hands still covered in flour she rushed down to the dock and prevented her daughters from going on board.[5] Ten years later the *Iroquois* foundered in a gale near Sidney, April 10, 1911, with a loss of fourteen lives, including the wife and son of Evan Hooson of North Pender Island.[6]

This marine accident, together with others closer to home, served to remind the Gulf Islanders of their tenuous relationship with the sea. The first recorded incident in Active Pass — the near grounding of H.M.S. *Termagant* at Laura Point — occurred in 1860.[7] During a heavy snowstorm in February 1872, the barque *Zephyr,* loaded with sandstone from Newcastle Island, struck Georgina Shoals and sank off the northeast coast of Mayne Island with the loss of two lives.[8] The construction of the Georgina Point lighthouse in 1884 considerably aided navigation through Active Pass, but Henry Georgeson had to cope with a manually operated foghorn until 1911, when the first automatic steam foghorn was installed. When balky machinery refused to start during heavy fog in the early years, Henry was forced to use a hand-operated horn to warn nearby ships entering Active Pass. Despite these extraordinary services, the CPR steamer *Princess Adelaide* went aground at Georgina Point, almost on the lighthouse doorstep, October 13, 1918.[9]

During another snowstorm in the record-breaking winter of 1915-1916, the 3,700 ton *Kenkon Maru #3* went aground on Belle Chain Reef near Bennett Bay. The ship had been bound for Vladivostok from Seattle with a cargo of railroad ties and knocked-down box cars.[10] The crew boarded with the Thomas Bennetts and William Deacons until the damage could be ascertained. Despite the fact that the ship's owners brought in a salvage crew from Japan, inclement weather hindered refloating the badly damaged ship for six months. The ship's captain added further drama to the marine accident by refusing to leave the island, and the federal government was forced to hold an inquiry on Mayne.[11]

The turbulent waters of Active Pass also claimed lives from time to time. John and Louisa Silva, who had developed the Village Bay farm that John and Margaret Deacon purchased in 1883, lost two of their children, John and Martha, about 1880, and moved to Gabriola Island to escape their sad memories. In two separate accidents in the 1930's,

Miners Bay, 1904, as seen from the deck of the Iroquois. *The only building not present in 1984 is the Mayne Island Hotel, on the left. PABC photo 25790*

Archie Deacon, age 22, and Lawrence Kirby and his friend, Allison Copland, were drowned.[12] A healthy respect for the sea and early training in navigation prevented the occurrence of many more tragedies in nearby waters.

* * * * *

The positive aspects of island living far outweighed the negative. An adequate ferry service enabled Gulf Islanders to continue catering to summer visitors, and to market agricultural produce in Victoria and Vancouver. A combination of low freight rates and property taxes allowed farmers to compete easily with producers on the mainland and Vancouver Island for the next fifty years. In 1902 seventy dozen eggs plus sheep, hogs and chickens were shipped weekly from Mayne to Victoria on the *Iroquois*. When the Vancouver public market opened in 1907, the Islanders welcomed this new outlet and requested Vancouver City Council to support adequate steamer connections with the Gulf Islands.[13]

About 1910 Richard Hall established Mayne Island's first hothouse industry, specializing in spring daffodils and tomatoes. After serving in World War I, Hall returned to Mayne Island, pioneered the use of doubled trussed greenhouses large enough (300'×40') to accommodate a team of horses and a plough, and became known as the "tomato king" among horticulturalists on the Pacific Coast. In 1921 his weekly shipments in the spring season amounted to 45,000 daffodils and one ton of tomatoes. He received a top price of $8 to $10 per twenty pound crate of early spring tomatoes in Vancouver. James Bennett and Hunter Jack also shipped tomatoes on a smaller scale, but, eventually, Japanese labourers employed by Hall and Bennett took over the hot house industry in the 1930's. The mild climate, which provided more sunshine than the Fraser Valley, ensured that Gulf Island tomatoes could reach Vancouver markets two or three weeks ahead of mainland competition. Unlike the Islanders' first attempts at

A gathering of residents from various islands at Galiano, ca. 1902, possibly on July 1st. Some of the people identified are:
Back row (1 to r) Jessie Georgeson, Bella Wright, Mrs. Winstanley, Dolly Page, George Watkinson, James Sinclair, Mrs. Sinclair, Jemima Georgeson, John
Aitken, Hunter Jack, Alice Bennett, Andy Georgeson, Gertie Jack, Johnny Georgeson, Mrs. Jack Sr.
Second row: Finlay Murcheson, Johnny Page, Darrel Sinclair, Bob Wright.
Front row: Harry Wright, Tilly Wright, Ellen Georgeson, Mary Bennett, Gertrude Sinclair, Stanley Robson.
Photo courtesy Mabel Nicholson.

A May 24th, 1902, gathering at Mayne Island, with Alice and Thomas Bennett at lower centre. Photo courtesy of Mabel Nicholson.

In pre-radio days musicians were in great demand. Albert Nicholson played the dulcimer when he and his family lived on Mayne Island between 1904 and 1919. Photo courtesy Mabel Nicholson.

fruit growing, which were defeated by the Okanagan market in the early 1900's, the hothouse industry remained viable until higher freight rates were introduced by the CPR shortly after 1950.[14]

When the Salt Spring Island Creamery opened in 1904, farmers on the other islands were encouraged to send cream there rather than to Victoria. From an early production of 30,000 pounds of butter a year, the creamery produced 140,000 pounds annually by 1928. Fred and James Robson on Mayne Island, and A. H. Menzies, Washington Grimmer and their sons on North Pender Island established registered Jersey herds, which supplied the Salt Spring enterprise. Farmers with smaller herds benefitted by selling milk to the creamery, too.[15]

Local farmers such as James Bennett and Albert Nicholson were successful at raising berry crops, especially strawberries. In 1922 a jam factory opened on Salt Spring which accepted shipments of fruit from the outer Islands, but inital production amounted to 500 cases only, and the operation soon terminated.[16]

The sedimentary formations of the Gulf Island contributed to small sandstone quarries on Salt Spring, Saturna and North Pender. Sandstone from similar formations on Newcastle Island found their way into the causeway at Victoria and the San Francisco Mint. In 1911 the Franco-Canadian Company built a brick plant at Bennett Bay, Mayne Island, to develop the deposit of blue clay which ran inland for one half mile on the Thomas Bennett farm. A large, Tudor-style boarding house was erected for the men, tracks laid for ore cars and a kiln built near a concrete barge landing. World War I closed the operation when funds dried up from the French interests.[17] A brick plant operated on North Pender, also, in 1910.

Vacation resorts continued to be popular among holidayers who enjoyed the trip by steamer to Miners Bay, and the individual attention received at the boarding houses and small hotels on Mayne Island. The splendid Point Comfort Hotel attracted such

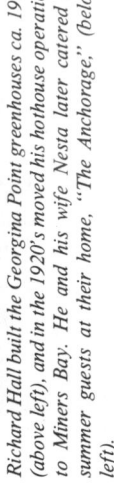

Richard Hall built the Georgina Point greenhouses ca. 1912 (above left), and in the 1920's moved his hothouse operation to Miners Bay. He and his wife Nesta later catered to summer guests at their home, "The Anchorage," (below left).

*The Mayne Island brick yard wharf, ca. 1914.
Jack Aitken photo.*

prominent families as the Bell-Irvings from Vancouver until the building reverted to a private residence about 1910.[18] The Deacon's boarding house at Village Bay, and the Mayne Island Hotel at Miners Bay operated until 1914 and 1923 respectively, when both buldings were destroyed by fire. The Mayne Island Hotel had grown considerably over the years from its modest beginnings as John Puetz's store in 1885. By 1923 it boasted a ballroom, billiard room, indoor plumbing and electric lights (from a generator).[19]

When Tom Collinson died in 1911 his daughter and her husband, Emma and Brook Naylor, took over the operation of his boarding house. Naming their new home Grandview Lodge, they set out to manage it in conjunction with a small farm. Boarders were treated to fresh garden vegetables, berry pies and home-made bread, and slept in beds furnished with hand-embroidered linens and home-made quilts of sheep's wool. Many of the Naylors' guests came because of the excellent fishing in Active Pass during the summer months. Mrs. Naylor, herself, enjoyed fishing and could often be seen rowing her guests about the bay on a summer evening. In 1930 the Naylors added a six-bedroom wing to the original building (one bedroom furnished ornately as a bridal suite), with indoor plumbing, a parlour, dining room and a large kitchen on the ground floor. Like the Mayne Island Hotel, it also acquired an electric generator for lighting, and for operating a large, walk-in refrigerator. The Naylors catered to as many as thirty guests a week during the summer. In 1934 the rates were $14.00 single and $12.50 double per week, all meals included.[20]

For those people who found the cost of a week's stay prohibitive, Sunday excursions were very popular during the summer months. Up to 700 people would arrive for a picnic in the park adjacent to Grandview Lodge, and afternoon tea was served in the dining room. Church congregations and companies such as Woodwards and Canadian Pacific in Vancouver, and Spencers in Victoria chartered the *Motor Princess* or other CPR vessels for their annual summer picnics. Publicity for these excursions was provided by writers such as Nellie McClung, who reported her impressions of a Sunday visit to Grandview Lodge in the 1930's for the *Winnipeg Free Press:* "In an old-fashioned dining room with point lace on the high shelf of the side-board, and pictures on the walls in carved wooden frames with leaves on the corners, we ate strawberry

50

On a leisurely Sunday Afternoon in the 1920's, picnickers return to their excursion ship after a visit to the park behind Emery's store, and possibly tea at Mrs. Naylor's Grandview Lodge (right). PABC photo 32852

Emma Naylor, centre, with summer employees Mr. and Mrs. Ewan, ca. 1935. Photo courtesy Margaret Bennett.

The Princess Royal *also served the Gulf Islands ca. 1930. Of wooden construction, she was scrapped in 1934. Photo courtesy G. Storey.*

shortcake and drank tea out of nice old English china."[21] Age and ill health finally forced Mrs. Naylor to curtail her hotel operations in 1943, although she was always ready to take in a stranded visitor.[22]

In 1936 Richard and Nesta Hall began operating their large home overlooking Active Pass and Miners Bay as a guest house, "the Anchorage." Vacationers there and from the Grandview Lodge cheerfully took part in social activities on the island, joining with local residents at the wharf on boat days, and dancing on Saturday nights at the community hall.[23] The Halls catered to vacationers until 1952, many of whom returned year after year. In addition, the Franco-Canadian boarding house, closed for so long at Bennett Bay, was operated as a hotel on a small scale between 1940 and 1950, and the Point Comfort Hotel, renamed the Cherry Tree Inn, reopened for a few years in the late 1940's before being permanently closed.[24]

* * * * *

The pleasant marine environment favored development of the hothouse and tourist industries, but it was also responsible for the arrival of the Eustace Maude family who introduced a British element to Mayne Island's agrarian society. Commander Maude had served on the Royal Navy ships *Scout, Rinaldo, Temeraire* and the Queen's private yacht, the *Victoria and Albert,* before retiring after twenty-one years of service. Maude homesteaded in Oregon, then moved to Duncan on Vancouver Island, where he operated a store, but he was never happy living away from the sea. In 1900 he re-established his family at Miners Bay where he bought waterfront property and carried on his drygoods business. When the Point Comfort Hotel was put up for sale about 1901, Maude moved his family into yet another waterfront home, at that time the most impressive building on Mayne Island. The Maudes operated their new home as a hotel in the summer time, and kept a small store and the bar open during the winter. About 1910 the family decided to give up serving the public, and the hotel reverted to the Maude's private residence.[25]

A very outgoing couple, with three daughters and a son (who later joined the Canadian Navy), Commander and Grace Maude frequently gave large parties and dances. Naval personnel from Vancouver and Victoria, together with English families from the other Islands, were invited to many of these affairs. The introduction of the gasoline launch by 1920 allowed a great deal of social intercourse among Island communities.[26]

Already the social center of the Islands for the farmers and early settlers, Mayne now became the focus of British middle-class activities. In addition to the parties and formal balls, tennis matches and afternoon teas were regularly held at Point Comfort during the summer. Occasionally, the sons and daughters of the agrarian community would be invited to these gatherings, but formal dances were more exclusive. In turn, Commander Maude accepted invitations from English families on Salt Spring and the other Islands, taking his family and guests on his sloop, the *Half Moon.* When Colonel and Lady Constance Fawkes arrived from England in 1924 they bought the Point Comfort

Tennis at Point Comfort. Photo courtesy Margaret Bennett.

A departure scene at Point Comfort wharf. Photo courtesy Nancy Rainsford.

Eustace and Grace Maude. Georgina Point lighthouse in background. Mary Ellen Georgeson photo.

Eustace Maude's boat, the Half Moon, *in which he set out to sail to England in 1925 at age seventy-seven. Photo courtesy Nancy Rainsford.*

Hotel from the Maudes and continued the tradition of afternoon teas and tennis parties into the late 1930's.[27]

Initially, the Maudes were the only British middle-class family on Mayne Island. They quickly made contact with English remittance families on South Pender, Saturna and Samuel. In 1904 Canon Paddon and his family took up permanent residence in the vicarage on Mayne Island,[28] and Richard Hall, who had trained as an agriculturalist on Guernsey, arrived about 1910.[29] Together, the Maudes, Paddons and Richard Hall formed the nucleus of the British element on Mayne Island until a number of other pensioned British servicemen arrived with their families following World War I. Captain J. N. Waugh, Captain A. B. Gurney, Captain H. L. Houlgate, Lieutenant-Colonel Charles Flick, Richard Steele and Herbert Foster were either veterans of the Boer War, World War I, or both. Also included in this English circle were the island's resident doctor, Christopher H. West, who had trained in London and retired from service with the Northwest Mounted Police in 1924, and his successor, Dr. Thomas E. Roberts, in 1935.[30]

This cohesive group of British families assumed an active role in community affairs. They were largely responsible for maintaining the Anglican church on Mayne Island, the men serving as wardens while the women organized a ladies auxiliary. Canon Paddon, who had worked so hard to see the church established on the island, was succeeded by Reverend R. H. Porter and his family. Porter was provided with a small gasoline launch and managed to conduct three services every Sunday — on Mayne, Galiano and North Pender. Occasionally, Sunday afternoon services would also be held at the Bennett residence on the southeast side of the island for people too elderly or remote to attend morning service at Miners Bay.[31]

Lady Constance Fawkes, owner of Point Comfort Hotel from 1924 until 1945. Photo courtesy John Borradaile.

Col. Lionel Fawkes (l) chatting with neighbour George Luden at the gates to Point Comfort. Mabel Foster photo.

The Fawkes, Porters and Wests, rather than the agrarian segment of the population, were instrumental in organizing the first agricultural fair on the island in 1925. Agricultural fairs had begun at Victoria in 1861, and soon were a feature in most communities. Despite long distances and awkward journeys by boat, residents of the Gulf Islands were keen participants and observers at many of these shows every year. Salt Spring Island inaugurated their fair in 1896, but Mayne Island became the first of the outer Islands to establish an annual fair, and residents from Galiano, North and South Pender, and Saturna usually attended and submitted entries. Most of the Mayne Island occidental and Japanese farming families enjoyed entering garden produce, flowers, farm animals, home cooking and fine art in competition with entries from the English sector who had small kitchen gardens only. The cooperation of the ferry companies, making special excursions and transferring entries from other islands, enabled the little fair to continue with few breaks until the present time.[32]

Colonel Fawkes and Mrs. Foster also encouraged the development of the fine arts on the island. Fawkes was a highly-skilled water-colorist, and enjoyed giving art lessons to the school children every Friday afternoon. Mrs. Foster had studied photography in Portugal and was also adept at painting and weaving, which she taught to residents on the island.[33]

The other distinctive social group on Mayne Island was the Japanese. (There were only about twelve Indians living on the Helen Point Reserve.) The Japanese tended to blend socially with the descendants of the original settlers because both groups earned their living by fishing or farming, and did not have pensioned incomes. Their children attended the local school in contrast to those of the Maudes, Paddons and Halls who

Although other doctors resided temporarily on Mayne Island, these two men are remembered for their dedication and long service. Above, Dr. Christopher H. West, formerly with the Royal North West Mounted Police, and, below, veteran of World Wars I and II, Dr. Thomas E. Roberts in his dispensary. Photos courtesy Mrs. C. West and Margaret Bennett.

were sent to private school or were tutored by private governesses. Japanese and non-Japanese worked side by side during harvesting, on community "bees" to care for the school and community hall, or on major tasks such as transporting steam boilers from the beach to a Japanese greenhouse. They also spent leisure time together at golf, badminton, dances and card parties at the community hall.[34]

In the 1920's, Colonel and Lady Constance Fawkes were allowed to act as sponsors for the group baptism of twelve Japanese children. Two Japanese weddings were performed in St. Mary Magdalene Church at Mayne Island, but apparently no Japanese burials took place in the church cemetery.[35]

British immigrants have been frequently credited by historians of British Columbia as providing the social foundations of our province, especially in Victoria and the Okanagan. The social structure of Mayne Island presents another settlement pattern: community organization had been forged by an egalitarian group of settlers before the British immigrants arrived on the scene after 1900. British notions of class distinction were not upsetting to the established community; their cultural contributions were also welcomed.[36]

* * * * *

With a secure economic and social foundation, the small community on Mayne Island weathered the unsettled decades from World War I to World War II without major difficulties. The economy of Mayne Island was not adversely affected by World War I because the older, established occidental and Japanese farmers remained on the island during the war period. Self-exiled patriots Eustace Maude and his son, George, and Richard Hall enlisted with the part-Indian descendants of the original settlers, Robert and Arthur Georgeson, and Frank and Frederick Heck. The Mayne Island Roll of Honour lists eighteen men, but at least five of these veterans did not arrive on the island until after the war. There were no Mayne Island casualties. North Pender lost six men; South Pender four, and Saturna, one. Those residents who remained behind were active in the Red Cross Society, holding regular teas, bazaars and other community activities to raise funds. The Mayne Island branch collected $1,076.48 in three and one half years, and the women donated large amounts of handiwork.[37]

Returning soldiers brought fresh ideas back to their communities after the war. Frank Heck's contribution was the island's first automobile in 1919. By 1922 there were seven cars on the island and other new technology was intruding. The first airplane visited the island in 1919, and in 1924 residents flocked to the community hall to hear the provincial election results on a new crystal set owned by Dalton Hill, the local storekeeper. Limited telephone service was available on the island by 1911, and in 1930 Mayne became the telephone headquarters for the outer Gulf Islands when a transmitting station was erected at Miners Bay.[38]

Health care also improved to the benefit of the growing number of older residents. A hospital was built on Salt Spring in 1914, and Mayne residents enjoyed the advantage of their first physician, a Dr. Kincaid, in the early 1920's, followed by Dr. Christopher

58

Mrs. Isabel Johnston (nee Milne) and the pupils of Mayne Island School, June 29, 1923. Photo courtesy Masao Adachi.

The second schoolhouse, built in 1894. Shown here in 1913, with teacher Winifred New. Photo courtesy Donald New.

New technology arrives at Miners Bay, ca. 1925. In the background, the Princess Adelaide *is docked on a summer excursion. Photo courtesy Margaret Bennett.*

One of the first trucks on Mayne, ca. 1925 — a 1908 or 1910 Ford. Photo courtesy Margaret Bennett.

Frederick and Frank Heck, sons of pioneer settlers Jacob and Catherine Heck, proudly enlisted in World War I. Mayne Island Museum photo.

West in 1924 and Dr. Thomas E. Roberts in 1935. These doctors also went to the other Islands for emergencies, or the patients would come to Mayne. Insulated from the mainland, most Islanders remained protected from major epidemics. The children were generally spared measles, mumps and chicken pox, which were an accepted part of urban childhoods.[39]

From time to time, visiting journalists predicted that the Gulf Islands were an area just waiting for development, but the economy and the limited resources of the Islands during the inter-war years prevented any large-scale endeavours. The Gulf Islands Board of Trade, formed in 1919 with representatives from all the Islands, attempted to secure better steamer service, telephone facilities, and medical care, but it appears to have ceased operation after 1923.[40] Two large projects promoted in the 1920's were cancelled because of the Depression: a T.B. sanitarium that was to have encompassed the entire Miners Bay area, and a large CPR hotel on North Pender.[41] A fish reduction plant on North Pender encouraged local fishing during the 1920's and 1930's Besides the hothouse industry, the only new enterprise of consequence on Mayne Island was a small cannery begun on Saturna by Mr. and Mrs. R. J. Steele and moved to Mayne in 1937. By 1948 production totalled 13,000 cases of canned beef stew and plum puddings, but the enterprise moved to the mainland in 1953 because of unreliable freight service.[42]

Newspaper accounts of leisure activities on the Gulf Islands during the inter-war period give the impression that life was nothing but a series of dances, golf matches, tennis parties and excursions to other islands during the summer. Winters were less lively but still marked by weekly card parties and monthly dances at the community hall. Only rarely was the pleasant, settled community thrown off guard by such unusual

Mabel Foster performs one of the more unusual duties of a Gulf Island farmwife. Photo courtesy Roland Foster.

Carrying on a tradition learned in her native Shetland Islands, Anderina (Mrs. William) Deacon spins wool from sheep raised on the Deacon's Hardscrabble Farm. Mabel Foster photo.

62

R. E. McNeill's store, Mayne Island, in 1926. This second store was built only a few yards up the hill from the wharf and the first store built by Tom Collinson in 1900. Photo courtesy Dorothy Edgecombe.

Dorothy McNeill and the interior of her father's new store. Photo courtesy Dorothy Edgecombe.

The white flag drops and they're off! Egg and spoon race, May 24, 1913. Jack Aitken photo.

events as Commander Eustace Maude's attempt to sail around the world to England in 1925, at the age of 77.[43]

Loyalty and tradition remained very important to the Islanders. New Year's Eve dances and the 24th of May holiday were inter-Island events held on Mayne as late as the 1940's. Initiated by the early settlers and supported, later, by the British families, May 24th was a major celebration on Mayne.[44] Mothers would pore over Eaton's catalogues months ahead, choosing new hats and clothing for the big day. Afternoon events, featuring foot races and water sports, were followed by a dance in the evening. In 1921 three hundred people from the Islands were in attendance for the afternoon, and 150 remained for the dance. This tradition was enhanced by a permanent display of loyalty to the Crown for the coronation of George VI in 1937. A hexagonal "coronation seat" was built near the wharf at Miners Bay and a copper beech planted in the enclosure. This seat became the center of outdoor gatherings on boat days for many years to come.[45]

When the new King George and Queen Elizabeth visited Victoria in 1939, the CPR steamship *Princess Mary* made a special excursion among the Islands to take residents to Victoria. Many Mayne Island residents also walked out to the end of Helen Point to wave as the royal pair sailed by on the S.S. *Prince Robert.*[46]

Life was indeed pleasant on the Gulf Islands during the 1920's and 1930's. Although the Depression affected the farmers and pensioned incomes of ex-servicemen, people generally found that they could live on a little less and still get by, because property taxes remained low and most families preserved garden produce, fish and venison to tide them over the winter. In December 1936, A. E. Craddock, a North Pender Island resident, compared the cost of living between the city and the Gulf Islands, giving a total cost of $66.28 per month for the city, versus $22.90 for the Islands. Nevertheless, few newcomers to the Islands remained during the inter-war years unless they were on pensioned income.[47]

* * * * *

A Typical Boat Day

For more than seventy-five years the boat day routine for Gulf
Islanders involved waiting for the ship's arrival, gathering on
the wharf to witness the comings and goings, then waiting again
for the mail to be sorted. (Above) James Waugh, Grace Maude
and Kathleen Waugh at the coronation seat, built in 1937, with
Edith and Kenneth Deacon in the background. (Left) From 1926
to 1945, H. L. Houlgate trundled the mail from the wharf to the
post office by wheelbarrow. Princess Mary at the wharf, ca.
1938. (Below) While Mrs. Naylor served afternoon tea, the
problems of the world were solved by (l to r) Frank Heck,
Dalton Deacon, Dr. Thomas Roberts and Dick Steel, as the mail
was sorted. ca. 1938. Photos courtesy Mabel Foster, Geof
Storey and Nancy Rainsford.

The attractive label of the Mayne Island Japanese hothouse co-operative.

The most industrious segment of the Mayne Island population between 1920 and 1940 were the Japanese. They had managed to establish themselves in British Columbia at the turn of the century by working hard, being adaptable and forming co-operatives. Certainly, the Mayne Island Japanese had all these positive attributes. The large poultry co-operative (50,000 hens) that they had formed earlier in the century had been superseded by a tomato growing co-operative in the early 1930's. Members of the Active Pass Growers Association had eight acres of tomatoes under glass and produced fifty tons of tomatoes a year. During the summer, hundreds of boxes of tomatoes were shipped every Tuesday, Thursday and Saturday to Vancouver markets, delaying the *Princess Mary* half an hour or more while loading took place.[48] In addition, a private sawmill supplied local lumber needs, a fish saltery at Dinner Bay employed both occidental and Japanese labour, and other Japanese fished independently in the waters around Mayne Island. A visiting journalist reported 8,000 pounds of cod were caught and dressed at Miners Bay for one shipment in 1934.[49] Without exact figures, one can only conjecture on the basis of photographs and verbal reports that the industrious Japanese were conducting more than 50% of the commerce on Mayne Island by 1940, yet represented one-third of the population.[50]

As Japan's foreign policy became more ominous in the 1930's, British Columbia members of Parliament brought out the time-worn accusations of lower standard of living and lack of assimilability to keep the Oriental question before Ottawa. They later added a third theme of protest, "peaceful penetration." Fear of fifth column activities eventually brought about the federal government's decision to evacuate the Japanese from the coastal area, following Pearl Harbor.[51] In the late 1930's, MacGregor Macintosh, Conservative MP for Nanaimo and the Islands, who in 1931 had spoken in favor of enfranchisement for Japanese veterans of World War I,[52] became the standard bearer

Ei Kadonaga's home at St. John Point (Horton Bay), as it looks today.

A visit to Mayne Island by the Japanese Consul in 1925. Photo courtesy of John Nagata.

Kumazo Nagata's extensive greenhouse complex, ca. 1940. Photo courtesy John Nagata.

A typical shipment of tomatoes during peak season from Kumazo Nagata's hothouses. Photo courtesy of John Nagata.

of those Conservatives who wanted the Japanese out of British Columbia. In an address to the Vancouver Centre Conservative Association in January 1938, Macintosh called for an immediate census, using Mayne Island as an example of Japanese incursion:

> ... in 1920 the population of Mayne Island was almost entirely white. Then the Japanese invasion started and today there is hardly a white man engaged in the Island's hot-house and field tomato trade. Practically all the fishing in surrounding waters is done by Japanese. The head man of Mayne Island Japanese is reported to be the brother of a Japanese admiral . . . There are more Japanese than white children in the Mayne Island school; the young men send to Japan for their wives and Mayne Island boys are serving their time in the Japanese Navy.[53]

Macintosh's reasons for the Japanese success in tomato growing were equally racist:

> Japanese live in crude cabins with practically no furniture ... A number of groups or families crowd in together. They all work, even women with babies strapped to their backs. There is no apparent wage scale, as all workers are in the so-called family. Youth and boys are evidently indentured to learn the business, and they are all at it, early and late. They live mostly on rice.[54]

Mayne Island was a strong Conservative constituency during the 1930's, with the Conservatives having almost twice as many voters as the next largest group, the Liberals, but they recognized the "politicking" in Macintosh's speeches.[55] One Mayne Island resident, Lieutenant-Colonel Charles Flick, was incensed enough to write letters to the editors of the Vancouver *Daily Province* and the Victoria *Colonist,* refuting the statements made by Macintosh, and warning of the consequences of rash utterances. A veteran of the Boer War and World War I, Flick predicted all too well what was to happen four years later:

> Some of the statements credited to Captain Macintosh are gravely in error. There is, so far as I can ascertain from the Japanese, no relative to a Japanese admiral on Mayne Island. No Japanese boys or young men have gone from the Island to serve in either the Japanese Army or Navy; one young man did go to Japan several weeks ago but he went to get a bride and is now back on his little holding here.
>
> The Japanese standard of living on Mayne Island is generally speaking at least equal to if not superior to that of Europeans engaged in similar pursuits. The Japanese children here are bright, intelligent, clean and exceptionally well nourished. The Japanese homes here are neat and scrupulously clean; and the inmates at once courteous, civil, hospitable and of excellent community spirit toward their fellow citizens . . . Idle and untrue utterances by politicians concerning Japan and the local Japanese cannot do other than breed ill-feeling which is to be deplored when one considers that the British Empire controls the destinies of

some 300,000,000 Asiatics. Now that Japanese and British patrols and outposts are daily face to face, fully armed, ill blood here may start something that Canadians would not care to see.[56]

As a result of Conservative propaganda, claiming that many Japanese were entering Canada illegally, Mackenzie King implemented a Board of Review, headed by Hugh L. Keenlyside, Department of External Affairs, assisted by RCMP District Officer Commanding, G. W. Fish, Vancouver, and District Superintendent of Immigration, F. W. Taylor, Vancouver. The final report by the Board stated that very few Japanese had entered Canada illegally in recent years. There were probably no more than 100 Japanese in Canada illegally in 1938. An RCMP check of the Japanese communities on both Mayne Island and Salt Spring Island found no illegal residents.[57]

Life went on quietly for the Japanese on Mayne Island in the years preceding Pearl Harbor, and there was visible evidence that they were becoming upwardly mobile. Bungoro Minamide was about to move his family into a new home, and Kumazo Nagata's son, John, who had completed his high school education in Vancouver, was starting his own tomato business at Campbell Bay, employing a more advanced technique of circulating hot water heating in his greenhouses. Then came December 7, 1941.[58]

Immediately after the Japanese attack on Pearl Harbor the Japanese on Mayne Island were affected by implementation of Mackenzie King's "moderate policy." King feared reprisals on those Canadians under Japan's control if word of unfair treatment by Canadian authorities got back to the Imperial Government. Thus, recommendations made by the Standing Committee on Orientals in British Columbia were introduced: Japanese were forbidden to fish or use vessels off the coast of British Columbia; short-wave radio receiving sets, radio transmitters and cameras were banned; enemy aliens were to be removed from protected areas. As a result, the Canadian Navy impounded all Japanese fishing boats in British Columbia. They towed the Mayne Island boats to the Fraser River in mid-December.[59]

This disturbing action followed the removal of four Japanese men from Mayne Island on the night of Pearl Harbor. In the early morning hours a Provincial Police officer had roused Fred Bennett from his bed, sworn him in as a deputy, and ordered him to take the police to the residences of the men they had listed. Bennett faced a terrible dilemma, because he was being asked to help round up some of his friends, yet the consequences, if he refused, might be harsh. The round-up took less than an hour. One man was arrested as he was making his way to stoke the fires in the starting house, which contained flats of tomato seedlings almost ready to set out in the greenhouses for the 1942 season. Car keys were seized for twenty-four hours so that families could not follow their men down to the Miners Bay wharf.[60]

Forrest E. LaViolette gives two instances of Japanese males who were evacuated early in 1942. The first was the internment, between December 9, 1941, and January 14, 1942, of thirty-eight persons "dangerous to security." Then, in mid-January, Mackenzie King announced that about 6,000 Japanese nationals between eighteen and forty-five years of age were to be removed from the defence area. The first group of one hundred men finally left Vancouver on February 23rd "after the RCMP had done some special rounding up and some special pleading with them."[61]

With the loss of the fishboats and now the young men, the Japanese on Mayne Island prepared to face the worst. Evacuation orders were published March 25, 1942, giving them scant time to settle their affairs. A limit of 150 pounds of luggage was placed on each family. Precious possessions were packed up or hidden away in walls, rafters and the ground. The custodian of alien property of the Gulf Islands, Gavin C. Mouat of Salt Spring Island, was notified of the visible property left behind.[62]

In the midst of this turmoil, Kumazo Nagata, Secretary of the Active Pass Growers Association, wrote to the British Columbia Security Commission on April 15, 1942, confirming that members of the co-operative were ready to evacuate, but expressing concern that as yet no one had been designated to look after the extensive hothouse operations once the owners had been evacuated. — Rather than deprive the fruit and vegetable markets that year, the Mayne Island Japanese had decided to plant their tomato crops as usual. — Nagata also put in a plea for the non-Japanese workers who had helped with the tomato industry over the years:

> At this time may we convey to you our opinion that those already in employment now be permitted to remain so while possible for them, as we do not wish to have their source of income deprived from them while the greenhouses are being operated by our successors. These persons, though not Japanese, have been our assistants for many years.[63]

The strong bond between non-Japanese and Japanese farmers on Mayne Island is evident in Nagata's letter. Charles Flick had reiterated his pro-Japanese stand in a letter to the *Colonist* January 1, 1942. He believed that Pearl Harbor was "solely due to slackness on the part of the military forces of the U.S.A.," and expressed the hope that the Japanese fishing boats would soon be returned to the Candian owners (i.e., not sold to American fishermen).[64]

Antagonism towards the Japanese on Mayne Island cannot be substantiated following Pearl Harbor, but residents of Galiano and North Pender Islands wrote negative letters to the newspapers. On the same page of the *Colonist,* beside Flick's letter of January 1, 1942, a letter was published from North Pender Island, titled "Civilian Protection":

> . . . Not knowing who amongst that alien people can be trusted, we should move them all into the interior and draft them to work in various industries, some on farms, some in mines and some in road construction. We are paying dearly now for our past pacifism, wistful thinking, procrastination, and ignorance.[65]

On Tuesday, April 21, 1942, the CPR steamship *Princess Mary* came for the fifty Japanese men, women and children who waited on the Miners Bay wharf. Most of the Mayne Island residents were in attendance to shake hands and wish them well. It was a sad time for all.[66]

A gathering of Japanese families at Kumazo Nagata's home, Miners Bay. (l to r) Back row: Cho Sumi, Shintaro Sasaki, Etsuo Minamide, Bungoro Minamide. Middle row: Koji Saga, Kumazo Nagata, Mineiche Minamide, Fumiye Minamide, Mrs. Mineiche Minamide, Yoshi Kadonaga. Front row: Mrs. Kikumatsu Sumi, Mrs. Jimmy Sumi, Mrs. Kumajiro Konishi, Mrs. Choichi Sumi, Masako Sumi, and two grandchildren of Mrs. K. Sumi. ca. 1935. Photo courtesy John Nagata.

A week after evacuation, the first tomatoes of the season, so optimistically planted by the Japanese, were picked by their Mayne Island friends and sent off to market. Nagata had contracted management of his greenhouses to a Vancouver grower, R. Mayers, for the 1942 and 1943 seasons. The other greenhouses on the island were managed by Chinese growers from Victoria for 1942, and thereafter by local residents. In all, between 150,000 and 200,000 pounds of tomatoes were harvested. The Mayne Island school lost seventeen Japanese school children. Classes limped along until June and then the school closed until September 1944 for lack of pupils.[67]

When resettlement away from the Pacific Coast was being implemented, many of the Mayne Island families were allowed to remain together. The Nagata, Sumi and Konishi families and several others went to Turtle Valley, near Salmon Arm, where they erected rough shacks of green lumber, hoping their stay would be temporary. The winter of 1942 was bitterly cold and the men could find only temporary employment on nearby farms. After two years the group broke up. The Nagata and Konishi families moved closer to Salmon Arm, but others went to Kamloops and Toronto. For two other Mayne Island Japanese the evacuation was doubly tragic. A fisherman from the island jumped overboard while being returned to Japan, and Bungoro Minamide died shortly after he reached the sugar beet farms of Alberta. He was only about forty years of age.[68]

Between February and July 1942 the Smith Committee, established by Order-in-Council PC 987, sold or leased most of the Japanese fishing boats and equipment taken into custody on the West Coast. In July the remainder was turned over to the Custodian of Alien Property in Vancouver.[69]

Legislation introduced by Ottawa in June 1942, allowed the Soldier Settlement Board to buy the abandoned property of the Japanese on Mayne Island and elsewhere in British Columbia. Several Mayne Island residents managed to keep the hothouse industry going on the island, renting the greenhouses from the Board, until returning veterans acquired the property after the War.[70]

Eventually, Gavin Mouat auctioned off the abandoned Japanese possessions on Mayne Island. Mouat had interests in the Gulf Island Ferry Company, which operated the motor vessel *Cy Peck* between Fulford Harbour, Salt Spring, and Swartz Bay on Vancouver Island. The auction on December 1, 1943, was turned into almost a holiday outing, with a special excursion sailing of the *Cy Peck* bringing Islanders from Salt Spring and North Pender Islands. Farm machinery, two trucks and more than 5,000 feet of lumber were disposed of, along with household effects and tools. Ironically, while the possessions of the Minamide family sold for a fraction of their value, the Mayne Island Red Cross raised the substantial sum of $50.79 during the day selling coffee and sandwiches.[71]

After the auctions were completed the Adachi family of Mayne Island wrote repeatedly to Gavin Mouat, insisting that some of their belongings were still in their home. Fred Bennett made numerous searches to no avail. Finally, in desperation he poked a hole in the ceiling. The belongings were all there, although some mice nests had been added. For a number of years the absent Japanese gave buried saki wine to a few Mayne Island friends as Christmas gifts. The recipients would be instructed by letter where to dig for their presents.[72]

By another Order-in-Council, PC 3797, in May 1944, the federal government made the buying and holding of land for the Japanese an offense.[73] After the war many of the Japanese wanted to re-acquire their holdings on Mayne Island, but no less a person than Major-General G. R. Pearkes, MP for Nanaimo and the Islands, added his voice to the many residents protesting the return of the Japanese to their previous homes:

> I represent a constituency in which the Japanese lived in their thousands before the outbreak of this war. When war came with Japan those residents were removed as a protective measure . . . The people of my constituency have realized the difference that there is now that the Japanese have gone, and whether the Japanese are made citizens of Canada or not the people of Vancouver Island and the people of the Gulf Islands do not want to see the Japanese move back to those areas. I have letters from individuals, from farmers, from fishermen, from employers of labour, from churches and organizations, all containing this plea: Do not let the Japanese come back to this territory after the war.[74]

In the early 1950's the Koyama family returned to Mayne Island, but only in the 1970's have other descendants of the Mayne Island Japanese bought property on the island. Unfortunately, none of the new generation lives on their forebearers' land.[75]

The Mayne Island Japanese joined with other groups in British Columbia to seek greater compensation for their property losses when an investigation was held by Justice Henry I. Bird in 1947, but the awards were minimal. The Torazo Iwasaki family, formerly of Salt Spring Island, later tried through the Exchequer Court and then the Supreme Court of Canada to obtain satisfaction for their land, which had been

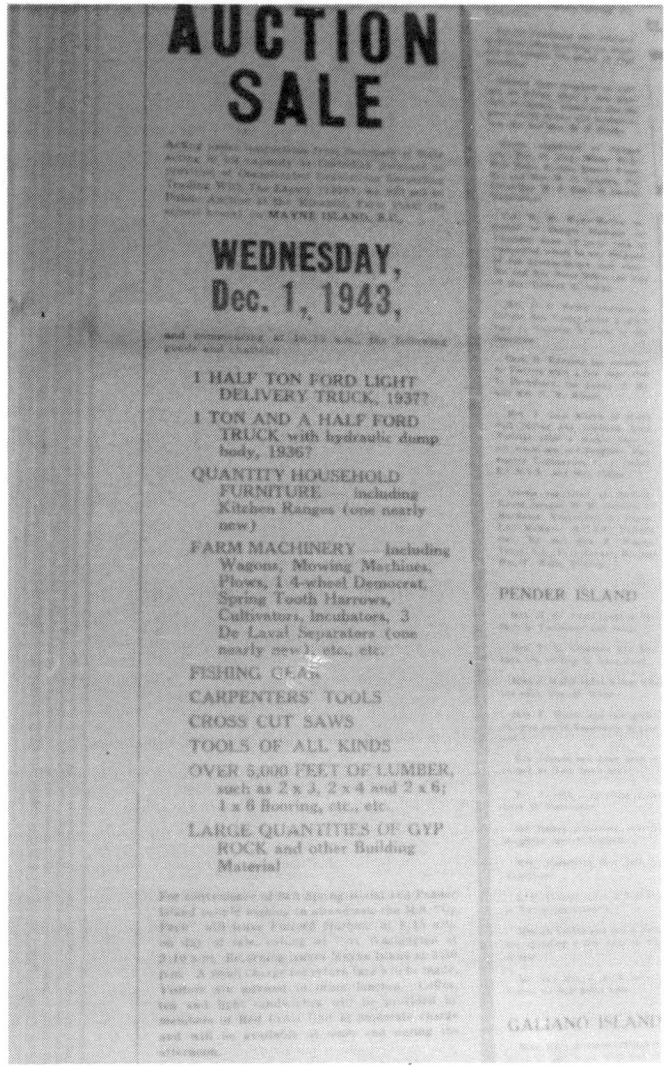

Notice of the auction sale held on Bungoro Minamide's farm in December 1943, from the Sidney Review.

A school gathering with trustee James Bennett, ca. 1941. Photo courtesy Margaret Bennett.

purchased by Salt Spring Lands Limited, a company in which Gavin Mouat, the custodian, held an interest. The courts refused both petitions, claiming that the acceptance of the award from the Bird decision was legally binding.[76]

Initially, the Mayne Island community was seriously affected by the evacuation of the Japanese. Although the results of Japanese labour, tomatoes, fish and (earlier) poultry, were sold off-island, and the Japanese worked through co-operatives to bring in chicken feed and hothouse supplies, the Japanese paid rent for their land and purchased their groceries from the local stores. These sources of income were now eliminated. Even the children's education was affected because of the school closure from September 1942 until September 1944. The community adapted in time to the loss of more than 30% of the population, nevertheless. Two grocery stores managed to remain in business, and hothouse tomatoes continued as a local industry until higher freight rates and lumber prices in the early 1950's made operating costs prohibitive. Thereafter, tomatoes were grown for local consumption only.[77]

* * * * *

The war touched Mayne Islanders in many other ways. While the sad fate of the Japanese on Mayne Island was being determined, wartime activities on the Islands were implemented. An area-wide blackout, including southern Vancouver Island, followed Pearl Harbor on the nights of December 8 and 9, 1941.[78] Civil defense groups organized area wardens to co-ordinate further blackout exercises, and the local newspaper, the *Sidney and Gulf Island Review,* published timely advice on measures to take should an

The militia group formed during W. W. II of residents from the outer Gulf Islands. ca. 1943. Photo courtesy Mary Ellen Harding.

incendiary bomb land on a roof. Two militia groups, one on Salt Spring and one from the outer Gulf Islands, held regular drills.[79]

The residents of Mayne Island raised money for war savings stamps by holding a lottery every Tuesday afternoon on the time that the *Princess Mary,* now painted in camouflage grey, would whistle for landing at Miners Bay. Annual victory bond drives went over the top every year, and dances, card parties and bazaars on Mayne and the other Islands were well attended, raising a considerable sum for the Red Cross. The Islanders endured rationing with little difficulty. Farm wives traded meat and butter coupons for the sugar coupons of non-farming women, and storekeepers earned everlasting respect for being generous with credit.[80]

For a short time the Royal Canadian Air Force stationed men at William Deacon's farm to retrieve drogues that were dropped in the fields during aerial target practices. An RCAF plane, unconnected with the operation, crashed on the south hills near Village Bay during the same time period, but there were no other military incidents on the island.[81]

After the war, Mayne Island welcomed home five returning veterans. The other Islands had a larger number of veterans and, unlike Mayne, had also lost men. Mayne Island's resident doctor, T. E. Roberts, who had survived Gallipoli in World War I, served as a ship's doctor on the H.M.S. *Awatea.* He resumed his practice on Mayne, and retired in 1951. He was aided in his work by Eva and Dick Steele who, in addition to operating the local cannery, were both trained nurses.[82]

By 1945 the social order on Mayne Island was changing. Not only had the Japanese departed, but many second generation descendants of the original settlers had died, as well as most of the British pensioned families, including matriarch Lady Constance Fawkes. Several young families moved to the island between 1945 and 1950, and more would come, if only temporarily, during the logging boom from 1948 to 1955.[83]

With the end of the War, residents of the Islands could once again focus on improvements to the community. Young mothers formed a Parent-Teacher Association in 1945 on Mayne Island, which sought better facilities for the school children. The Association purchased property for a new playground, and a new school was built on it in 1950.[84] In 1948 representatives from the Islands attended a Salt Spring Island Joint Council meeting to discuss the implementation of hydro service, and air and water transportation problems. This meeting marked the formation of the Gulf Islands Improvement Bureau, which would play such an important part in the history of the Gulf Islands during the next decade, especially in connection with obtaining adequate ferry service.[85]

The Canadian Pacific Railway had enjoyed a virtual monopoly of steamship service to the Gulf Islands since the 1920's. After employing a series of older ships and replacements, the company came to rely on the *Princess Mary* year round, supplemented by the *Motor Princess* during the summer months. Personalized service was still available as earlier in the century. Ships' officers accepted letters for posting on board ship if the local postmaster had already sealed the mailbags, and special calls were made to pick up members of a wedding party or to bring visitors to the annual fall fair. The Gulf Island Ferry Company occasionally brought the *Cy Peck* on excursion trips to Mayne and the other Islands on special days, too.[86] Unfortunately, while the *Cy Peck* continued operating for many more years, the days of the *Princess Mary* were numbered.

In 1949 the CPR eliminated Victoria from the *Princess Mary* run, which meant that the Gulf Islanders would have contact with Vancouver Island during the summertime only. At a meeting of the Gulf Islands Improvement Bureau in January 1950, George Pearkes, now MP for Saanich and the Islands,[87] agreed with the delegates that the Islands had less transportation than in earlier years. He felt that the federal government should be involved because they provided $3 million to aid Atlantic Coast steamships, but only $300,000 for West Coast marine transportation.

Protests and meeting with CPR officials failed to persuade them to provide more frequent service.[88] Little did the Islanders realize that they would still be struggling to obtain adequate marine transportation ten years later.

The most popular ship on the Gulf Islands run was the Princess Mary. *When the CPR finally withdrew her from service in 1951 the islanders felt they had lost a faithful friend. Mabel Foster photo.*

Formerly the Island Princess, *the* Cy Peck *began operating in 1931 between Fulford Harbour, Saltspring Island, and Swartz Bay, Vancouver Island, but she later served the outer Gulf Islands in the 1950's. Mabel Foster photo.*

Thirty years ahead of her time, designed for automobiles rather than passengers, the Motor Princess *was a summertime addition to the Gulf Island run in the 1930's. "Mothballed" because of stringent fire regulations in 1950, she was bought from the CPR by the Gulf Island Ferry Co. and reactivated in 1956. Mabel Foster photo.*

Only a shadow of her former self, the Motor Princess *served the Gulf Islands as the* Pender Queen *in the 1960's. Photo courtesy B. C. Ferry Corporation.*

A typical scene in late August at Miner's Bay in the 1950's. Mabel Foster photo.

Felix and Emma Jack of the Helan Point Reserve, ca. 1950. Photo courtesy Amelia Georgeson.

4

A DECADE OF DISRUPTION: 1950-1960

The ensuing ten years of disrupted passenger and freight service to the Gulf Islands taxed the patience of islanders and politicians alike. Individual islands, and even the residents of one island, were divided politically. Throughout this turbulent period, as the era of relaxed travel, focusing on passenger service, was being replaced by more rapid transit, favoring the automobile, the provincial government never fully understood the strong relationship between Mayne and Galiano Islands and the mainland, believing that most Gulf Islanders preferred marine connections with Vancouver Island.

When new, stringent fire regulations forced the retirement of the *Motor Princess* in May 1950, the aging *Princess Mary* took over her Sunday run. Rumours had been circulating for three years that the *Mary* would not last much longer because the ship was frequently pulled off the Islands route for boiler and engine repairs. In late 1951 the blow finally came. The CPR announced that the *Mary* would make her final run and be replaced by the *Princess Elaine* on December 13th. The *Mary* was eventually sold for restaurant and barge purposes; refitting would have required the costly removal of her entire superstructure to replace the boilers.[1]

The *Elaine* was 43 feet longer than the *Mary,* and required larger docking facilities and a larger passenger and freight business to make her operation viable, but the CPR had no other ships available. The company had recently added two luxury vessels, the *Princess Marguerite* and the *Princess Patricia* to their fleet and was not prepared to spend another $1 million on a smaller ship for the Gulf Islands run. Unfortunately, only Ganges on Salt Spring and Port Washington on North Pender had large enough wharves to accommodate the *Elaine.* The larger ship's schedule was thus much poorer than the *Mary's* had been. Whereas the *Mary* had called at every island except South Pender on Tuesday, Thursday and Saturday, the *Elaine* docked only at Ganges and Port Washington on those days. Mayne was serviced by the smaller west coast CPR steamer *Princess Maquinna* every eight days when she made her trip via Victoria to Vancouver and return.[2] Obviously, the increased business required by the *Elaine* was impossible to achieve.

To cries of protest from the Gulf Island Improvement Bureau, the CPR replied that the Islanders would have to press the federal government for new wharves before Mayne, Galiano and Saturna could receive better service. The CPR also suggested that these wharves be built with moveable ramps to facilitate side loading.[3] The Bureau immediately wrote to Alphonse Fournier, Minister of Public Works, Ottawa, December 27, 1951, pointing out that service once every eight days would ruin not only the hothouse and field produce business, but the tourist industry as well. It recommended improving the smaller wharves immediately.[4]

The federal government responded quickly to this plea, announcing in March 1952 that $557,500 would be spent on upgrading wharf facilities. Mayne Island's wharf at Miners Bay was ready for the *Elaine* on June 28th,[5] and wharves at Galiano, Saturna and Sidney also received instant attention. The *Elaine* was calling on all the Islands in the summer of 1953, completing round trips four times weekly between Vancouver and Sidney, but in September the CPR announced that it was going to pull the *Elaine* off the Gulf Islands run and provide a reduced service once a week, using the *Princess Norah.* A forty-hour work week and higher pay rates had added $308,000 to the operating costs of the CPR's British Columbia coast service in 1953. Expenditures for the first half of the year had exceeded revenues by $1,166,573, and two thirds of a $115,000 deficit on the Gulf Islands and Powell River runs was attributable to the Gulf Islands service. Each winter trip had cost $1,566 but revenues amounted only to $318. Furthermore, the crew numbered fifty, while the number of passengers on the winter run to the Gulf Islands averaged only forty-five.[6] The report neglected to publish revenues for the summer months when the CPR carried far more passengers, nor did it add that the *Elaine* could be gainfully employed on her old service, the Nanaimo-Vancouver run. Increasing traffic on that route was proving more than the *Princess of Nanaimo* could handle.[7]

Once again, protests were mounted against reduced service to the Islands. Jean Howarth, a weekend resident of Saturna, criticized the CPR's handling of the *Elaine* in a Vancouver *Province* editorial:

> . . . they must have known that she would lose money, and known that they intended to pull her off . . . But they let the taxpayers of Canada spend $500,000 on wharves that only the *Elaine* needs. The old wharves would have done quite well for the small ships now to be assigned to the run.[8]

The same day the Victoria *Colonist* editorialized, "As far as transportation services are concerned, the forgotten people of British Columbia are the settlers, businessmen and resort operators of the Gulf Islands."[9] As a result of the inadequate service, Mayne Island's cannery was moved to Vancouver in 1953.[10]

The Gulf Islands Improvement Bureau met and decided to seek restoration of service by writing to federal and provincial members and boards of trade, and by sending a delegation to interview vice-president William Manson of the CPR. Meanwhile, offers were received from Oswald "Sparkie" New of Coast Ferries Ltd., Vancouver, and from Gavin Mouat of the Gulf Island Ferry Company to supply a replacement service.[11]

When the CPR withdrew service to the Gulf Islands, the Lady Rose *served as the Islands' link with the mainland until she was replaced by the* Island Princess *in 1958. Marie Elliott photo.*

Following the visit from the Improvement Bureau delegation, the CPR reluctantly agreed to increase service from one to three times weekly during the winter of 1953-54. The *Princess Norah* and the *Princess of Alberni* were placed on the Gulf Islands route.[12]

In October, 1953, the CPR made known its plans for the summer of 1954. The *Elaine* would be used again, commencing June 1st, with stops at Galiano three days each week, and at Port Washington and Mayne twice a week. The *Norah* and *Alberni,* travelling in opposite directions to Victoria and Vancouver, would call on Wednesdays.[13] This piecemeal schedule suggested that the long tradition of CPR service to the Gulf Islands was coming to an end. Furthermore, by this time, the CPR was facing strong competition from Black Ball Lines-Canada Limited and was concentrating its efforts on retaining service between Nanaimo and Vancouver, and Victoria to Port Angeles and Seattle.[14] A number of delegations from the Gulf Islands Improvement Bureau and other interested groups met with Deputy Minister of Highways Evan Jones, requesting government intervention to ensure a year-round service. These groups also met with Black Ball Lines who promised to make an economic survey.[15]

When Sparkie New offered to provide a thrice-weekly service to the Islands from Steveston with the S.S. *A. G. Garrish* (later renamed the *Lady Rose),* the CPR was more than willing to allow New to take over the Gulf Islands route, promising to help with delivery of vehicles because the *Garrish* could transport only two cars. The little ship commenced sailing to the Gulf Islands on February 25, 1954. It also acquired the mail contract for the Islands.[16] New provided service to the Islands on a free enterprise basis but soon faced competition from the Gulf Island Ferry Company, which was subsidized by the provincial government to operate the *Cy Peck* between Fulford Harbour and Swartz Bay and, later, the *George Pearson* between Vesuvius Bay, Salt Spring Island and Crofton.

On February 24, 1954, a major attempt was made to gain government intervention when a large delegation (comprised of representatives from the Chambers of Commerce of Duncan, Victoria, Sidney and North Saanich; representatives from the Gulf Islands; Larry Giovano, MLA for Nanaimo and the Islands, and John D. Tisdale, MLA for Saanich) met with Philip A. Gaglardi, Minister of Highways. To a formal request for subsidized ferry service to all the Gulf Islands, Gaglardi replied that he was waiting for the economic survey then being carried out by Black Ball Lines before he made any decisions. This survey, which would have meant Black Ball acquiring the Gulf Island Ferry Company, was never made public despite repeated attempts by Gulf Islanders to learn the contents.[17]

Negotiations between the Gulf Island Ferry Company and Black Ball broke down in November 1954, but in the meantime the Salt Spring ferry company introduced a new run of the *Cy Peck,* from Fulford Harbour to North Pender Island and Swartz Bay in October 1954. Delegates from the outer Islands visited Evan Jones October 28, 1954, requesting that the *Cy Peck* be subsidized to serve their communities, too, but this request was turned down, even with the support of written submissions from the Islanders, including this poem from Mayne's senior "poet," Jimmy Neill:

To the Honorable P. A. Gaglardi —

I have been told you are the man
To study our petition,
And try to help us all you can
In our present sad position.
Our government was kind to us
For to build a nice new wharf,
With lots of room for landing,
Ramps to take cars on and off.
Things have changed here for the better;
Our hotel may open up
For to take in lots of visitors
And that should bring us luck.
The *Lady Rose* is rather small
When the wintery breezes blow.
She sure can shake your stomach up
'Tho safe enough, you know.
A short route to Victoria
From Mayne is what we need
To take on cars and passengers;
That would help us out indeed!
If you would use your influence,
Soon our Island would expand.
We will thank you for your kindly help;
Then, this Island would be grand.[18]

Aided by the completion of a bridge linking North and South Pender Islands in March 1955,[19] traffic on the North Pender Island-Swartz Bay route increased fifty per cent between October 1954 and October 1955. Increasingly, residents of Salt Spring and North and South Pender Islands were forging links with Vancouver Island as automobile and freight volumes grew. In opposition were Galiano, Mayne and Saturna residents who believed that their future lay in closer contact with the mainland. In November 1954 they met with Jones again in an attempt to gain additional service for the Islands, not a replacement for the existing mainland connection via the *Lady Rose.* Differences in opinion led to the withdrawal of the Pender Island Farmers Institute from the Gulf Island Improvement Bureau in November 1954. Thenceforth, the Institute began to promote stronger ties with Vancouver Island, while the Bureau, now composed of Galiano, Mayne and Saturna representatives, promoted mainland connections.[20]

At a large meeting of representatives from all the Islands on Galiano in May 1955, Evan Jones suggested they "get their act together" if they wanted better ferry service. Both Gavin Mouat and Sparkie New presented their opposing viewpoints, Mouat favoring subsidized ferries, and New favoring free enterprise. A subsequent meeting on Mayne Island in May revealed that the residents wanted a government study of the ferry situation, but were divided on subsidy and route questions.[21]

The Gulf Island Improvement Bureau held a plebiscite in September 1955, asking the residents of Mayne, Galiano and Saturna to choose between subsidized car ferry service to Vancouver Island or a general freight and passenger service to the mainland. Eighty per cent of the Galiano residents and ninety per cent of the Mayne and Saturna residents responded. The majority, 391, preferred a mainland service, and 114 preferred the subsidized car ferry service to Vancouver Island. Pender Island refused to hold a similar plebiscite but submitted a petition to the provincial government signed by 218 residents, requesting continuation of the existing subsidized service.[22]

There is no evidence that a study was carried out during 1955 on the best method of servicing the Gulf Islands. Gaglardi does not seem to have understood that more than half the Gulf Island residents favored connections with the mainland, despite the plebiscite results which were forwarded to him by New. In December 1955 Gaglardi finally announced that the provincial government would immediately subsidize service to the outer Gulf Islands by the *Cy Peck,* connecting with Swartz Bay. New's request that the government withdraw their subsidies to Mouat and allow him to compete freely with the Salt Spring company were ignored. New claimed that Coast Ferries had made an 18% profit on the Gulf Islands run between December 1954 and December 1955.[23]

When the government called tenders for service to the Gulf Islands in early 1956, the sole response was from Mouat's Gulf Island Ferry Company, which requested an annual subsidy of $84,000 over five years, commencing July 1956.[24] Gaglardi accepted the tender with the provision that the Company provide twice daily service to the outer Islands during the summer, and once daily service in the winter.[25] The *Motor Princess,* which Mouat bought from the CPR in January 1955, was refitted promptly and began her inaugural run on June 29, 1956, with Premier W. A. C. Bennett and Gaglardi on board. Bennett assured the Gulf Islanders that,

This trip which I have taken with Mr. Gaglardi means that the government of British Columbia is recognizing the new importance of the Gulf Islands and we intend to vigorously proceed with policies that will increase this development.[26]

The early settlers initially relied on oxen rather than horses for farm work. Babe was the last ox on Mayne Island, seen here with owner Roy Aitken, ca. 1955. Mabel Foster photo.

William Deacon's steam engine, brought to the coast in 1885, and to Mayne about 1900, was used by island farmers until 1949. It is now at the Saanich Pioneer Museum. (l to r) Wilbert Deacon and John Bennett. Photo courtesy Caroline Hopton.

A threshing scene on Stanley Robson's farm, ca. 1950. Photo courtesy of Margaret Bennett.

Jack Aitken making hay, ca. 1935.
Mabel Foster photo.

With a provincial election looming, Bennett sent a personal letter to Gaglardi, July 9, 1956, asking that special attention be given to the Gulf Island problems.[27] As a consequence, the Gulf Islands were better served than ever before, with daily connections via either the *Motor Princess* or the *Lady Rose* to Vancouver Island and the mainland, and Earle Westwood, Social Credit candidate for Nanaimo and the Islands, easily won the Gulf Island vote in the election that September.[28]

In late 1956 New reversed his position on free enterprise and requested a subsidy of $3,000 a month for the *Lady Rose* or he would have to withdraw the ship from service in January 1957. His change of stance was likely caused by rapidly increasing operating costs, especially wages. The Gulf Islands Improvement Bureau unanimously endorsed New's request. Acting on the advice of Earle Westwood, Gaglardi provided New with $500 monthly subsidy for one year and consulted with George Paulin, President of Black Ball Ferries Ltd., regarding his company's interest in supplying service to the Gulf Islands. Paulin proposed that if the government would purchase the Black Ball ferry terminal in Victoria for $700,000 and grant an exclusive franchise for a period of 25 years for a Gulf Island service, Black Ball would purchase the Gulf Islands Ferry Company for $370,000, the payment to be spread over ten to fifteen years, and take over all the Gulf Islands terminals. Such a proposal was clearly unacceptable, and Gaglardi chose instead to maintain the status quo.[29] When a delegation from Saturna, Mayne, Galiano and North and South Pender formally requested him on February 11, 1957, to provide permanent transportation services to Vancouver with a larger vessel than the *Lady Rose,* Gaglardi insisted that such a service would be uneconomical and that Gulf Island development was "tied tightly" to Vancouver Island rather than the mainland. The delegation managed only to extract the usual promise that he would consider having another survey done.[30]

* * * * *

The difficulties with ferry transportation were reflected in the decrease in population of the outer Gulf Islands. The population of North and South Pender, Mayne and Saturna dropped from 742 in 1951 to 592 in 1956, a decrease of 20%, and Galiano and Valdes dropped from 587 to 535, a decrease of 9%. Only Salt Spring, which had enjoyed uninterrupted ferry service with Vancouver Island since 1932, registered a slight increase of 2%. Cessation of the brief logging boom in the Gulf Islands accounts for part of the population decline but not all of it, because most of the logging crews were formed from local residents.[31]

From 1957 onwards the residents of the Gulf Islands began to press for provincial government takeover of the Gulf Island Ferry Company, a change in stance from their initial requests for mere subsidization. The government took five years before complying with the new proposition.

Delegations and meetings of outer Gulf Islands residents, often including the Salt Spring Chamber of Commerce, began in September 1957 to press for takeover of the Gulf Island Ferry Company to ensure over-all, efficient management.[32] Ferry traffic

Except for the use of electric clippers, the technique of shearing sheep has never changed for Mayne Island farmers such as Fred Bennett. Margaret Bennett photo.

Ceremonies on the Mayne Island wharf to mark the inaugural service of the Island Princess *in September 1958. Sparkie New with Fred Bennett and William Wilks at centre. Marie Elliott photo.*

increased considerably for the Gulf Island Ferry Company between January 1957 and January 1958; vehicles rose from 296 to 354 and passengers from 567 to 857. The time-wasting run through Active Pass to Sturdies Bay, Galiano, and Miners Bay, Mayne Island, was eliminated when the provincial government completed end-loading wharves at new dock sites in Montague Harbour and Village Bay at a cost of $124,000.[33]

Subsidies continued to Coast Ferries Ltd. until that company decided to build a new ferry. In June 1957 Gaglardi announced an additional subsidy of $7,000 to cover the period June to October, but New was not happy and suggested that fares would have to be increased. A further subsidy of $2,000 for the winter months of November 1957 to February 1958, for three trips weekly, was also granted.[34]

With the backing of outer Gulf Islands residents who were willing to become shareholders in the enterprise, New next formed Gulf Island Navigation Company Ltd. which commissioned a 20 vehicle, 300 passenger ferry, the *Island Princess.* The new ferry replaced the *Lady Rose* in September 1958,[35] thus giving Mayne Islanders two ferry services six times a week. Then, after a crippling strike by the CPR left Vancouver Island almost cut off from the mainland, Premier Bennett announced at the end of 1959 that Swartz Bay would become the terminal for a new B.C. ferry fleet.[36]

The first half of 1960 was marked by disarray among Gulf Island groups as they separately and jointly submitted briefs calling for provincial takeover of the Gulf Island service. Pender began the year by petitioning for a 50-60 car ferry with a 350 passsenger capacity, plus a bridge between Saturna, Samuel and Mayne. Sparkie New presented a brief from Gulf Island Navigation Company to the Executive Council in February asking the government to withdraw subsidies to the Salt Spring based Gulf Island Ferry Company, predicting an annual 5% increase in traffic. In May a delegation of Salt Spring businessmen from the Chamber of Commerce and the Businessmen's Association asked the government to absorb the Gulf Island Ferry Company into its Department of Highways operations.[37]

In July all the Islands finally united in a plea to the government to take over the ferries: Chambers of Commerce on Salt Spring, Pender and Galiano were joined by the Mayne Island Farmers Institute. Saturna was polled and seventy-five per cent voted in agreement. At a cabinet meeting held at Harbour House, Salt Spring, July 20, 1960, the Islanders presented further briefs, as did Sparkie New. Saturna, while agreeing to the government takeover, did not want the *Motor Princess* and *Cy Peck* to become part of the government fleet. Their petition complained that these two ships were too old and slow and suggested two faster ferries to operate from Swartz Bay. The Chambers of Commerce brief argued that open-ended ferries were similar to highways, and because ferry operations had now expanded beyond the capacity of private enterprise, the government should assume this obligation. New stubbornly clung to his belief in free enterprise, insisting that his new ferry had made 9½% interest on common stock, and that the provincial government should get out of ferry operations.[38]

The summer traffic in 1960 was handled well by the *Motor Princess* and the *Island Princess,* the latter making two round trips on Sundays to return weekenders to the mainland, especially from Galiano, Mayne and Saturna.[39] In October ferry service switched to a winter schedule, but the *Motor Princess* continued to serve the Islands every day, while the *Island Princess* eliminated the Monday and Wednesday trips to Islands.[40] With this satisfactory service it is difficult to understand why Gaglardi asked his former Deputy Minister, Evan Jones, now retired, to investigate service to the Islands in late October 1960. Jones' findings resulted in the *Motor Princess* being replaced by the smaller *Cy Peck* for the winter months. Chambers of Commerce on Pender, Galiano and Salt Spring were again joined by the Mayne Island Farmers Institute in sending telegrams of protest to Premier Bennett. In January 1961 these groups jointly requested the government to act on their last petition of July 1960, which had asked for government takeover of the Gulf Island Ferry Company. Jones revised his report and allowed the *Motor Princess* to serve the outer Islands on Mondays, but cars were still occasionally left behind at Mayne and Swartz Bay.[41]

When the B.C. ferries commenced operations at Swartz Bay in 1960, business from Ganges fell off sharply for the *Island Princess*. The Gulf Island Navigation Company dropped Ganges, adding Sidney to the *Island Princess* route four times weekly, commencing in March 1961.[42] New sought permission to use the new ferry docks at Tsawwassen to shorten the travel time for the *Island Princess,* but the government refused his request.[43] In May, Gaglardi suggested to New that the Gulf Island Navigation Company buy out the Gulf Island Ferry Company, or vice versa. The latter was not interested, but New offered to pay the Gulf Island Ferry Company their 1961 insurance assessments of its ferries plus five years' profit. The Gulf Island Ferry Company turned down the offer, and in June 1961 Earle Westwood announced that the provincial government finally planned to acquire the Gulf Island Ferry Company.[44]

In the light of this proposed government action, New immediately announced that he would cancel the *Island Princess* run to the Gulf Islands, September 11, 1961.[45] Another strong protest was registered by the Islanders who were now joined by a group of residents from Vancouver who had bought retirement property on the Islands and, in the meantime, had become weekend commuters. They met with Westwood on Galiano July 30th, then with Gaglardi on August 28th. In response to their petition, which stated that elimination of the *Island Princess* would have adverse effects on land values, land development, local industry, mail service and summer visitors, Gaglardi agreed that the service to the Gulf Islands from the mainland was inadequate and promised to recommend a subsidy to the cabinet. Nothing came of this promise.[46]

A cheque for $250,000 was handed over to Gavin Mouat by Premier Bennett at the Swartz Bay terminal, September 1, 1961. The British Columbia Toll Highways and Bridge Authority had now officially acquired the *Motor Princess, Cy Peck* and *George S. Pearson* from the Gulf Islands Ferry Company after seven long years of petitions, pleas and demands from Gulf Islands residents, but their transportation problems were still far from settled.[47]

In October 1961, New requested that the provincial government purchase the *Island Princess* outright or provide a subsidy of $4,000 a month to allow the Gulf Island Navigation Company to break even. New pointed out that Pender and Saturna traffic had declined because of the Gulf Island Ferry Service, but that Mayne and Galiano still needed a link with the mainland. He suggested bridging Mayne to Samuel and Saturna, allowing a Tsawwassen to Swartz Bay ferry to call at Beaver Point on Saltspring, Port

Washington on North Pender, and at Mayne and Galiano.[48] When the government did not respond to his request, New took the *Island Princess* off the Gulf Island route on November 15, 1961, and placed her on a northern service, based at Kelsey Bay. The ship never returned to Gulf Island waters.[49]

For the next year and a half commuters from the mainland to Galiano, Mayne, North and South Pender and Saturna had to take a B.C. ferry to Swartz Bay, sailing past their island homes, in order to transfer to the smaller *Motor Princess,* which in turn would retrace half the route they had just covered to deliver them to their destinations. The "medieval process" took five hours of ferry time to cover a normal commuting distance of fifteen to twenty miles — time enough, the mainlanders complained, to fly 3,000 miles to Toronto. They further claimed that with the cessation of the *Island Princess,* transportation service to the Islands was set back sixty years.[50]

Why were requests for adequate ferry service to the Gulf Islands handled in such a cavalier fashion by the Department of Highways? Two factors are obvious. The Gulf Islands were still lightly populated in the 1950's compared to the lower mainland and the Okanagan where huge projects, the Deas Island tunnel thruway and the Okanagan highway, were under construction. Secondly, there were also highway projects under way on the John Hart Highway between Prince George and Dawson Creek, and on the Yellowhead route btween Prince George and Prince Rupert. All these contracts required enormous amounts of money and attention.[51] The Gulf Islanders' petitions and meetings with government officials were of minor consequence compared to developments elsewhere in the province demanding supervision by the Highways Department.

* * * * *

The problem of ensuring adequate ferry service was merely one aspect of life on the Gulf Islands during the late 1950's and early 1960's. Assessments on the Islands rose from $6.5 million to more than $10 million between 1958 and 1962, yet the government share of the school costs was reduced from 58% to 19.5%. This reduction meant that local taxpayers had to make up the difference. To help pay their taxes three elderly owners on Mayne Island subdivided their large farms in 1960-61. Because of these subdivisions and similar ones on the other Islands, there were three times as many taxpayers in 1961 owning property on the Gulf Islands — in Mayne Island's case, four times — than there were in 1941.[52] Many of these new owners were mainland residents who had bought lots for investment, vacations or retirement purposes.

Hydro service, introduced on south Galiano and Mayne in December 1956, was completed to North Pender and Saturna in 1961.[53] South Pender and north Galiano remained without service for several more years. After many plebiscites a new hospital at Ganges was approved and it opened in April 1958.[54] The old hospital became a boarding home for outer Islands high school students attending the only high school for the Gulf Islands at Ganges.

The one new industry introduced in the outer Gulf Islands between 1950 and 1960 was an aggregate shale plant on Saturna in 1959. Similar plants operated at Beaver Point and Long Harbour on Salt Spring Island for a number of years.[55] Several oil companies expressed an interest in the possibility of petroleum resources, but exploratory drilling by Shell Canada in 1963 revealed that the strata had been laid down too rapidly, thus preventing good reservoir conditions for oil entrapment.[56]

During this same time period new residents and weekend commuters brought changes in the social organization of the island. With cessation of the *Island Princess* service in 1961, residents of Mayne Island no longer had a reason to gather on boat days at Miners Bay to share the latest news. Commuters found accommodation only for their cars at the efficient, traffic-oriented terminal at Village Bay. When new owners refurbished the old Grandview Lodge (renamed Springwater Lodge) at Miners Bay and the Franco-Canadian boarding house at Bennett Bay (renamed the Arbutus Lodge, then Mayne Inn) with liquor lounges, these hotels became informal social centers where oldtimers, new residents, weekenders and visitors could become acquainted.[57]

While the government and private interests ignored their plight, Islanders and commuters had no choice but to ride out the storm regarding transportation to the mainland. Future years would prove that this seemingly difficult period was actually the lull before the storm created by unprecedented growth and environmental change. During the next twenty years, Mayne Island and the rest of the outer Gulf Islands were reluctantly, but relentlessly drawn into the Georgia Strait urban region, bounded by Vancouver, Nanaimo, Victoria and Seattle.[58]

Springwater Lodge, Miners Bay, 1984.

The Mayne Inn, Bennett Bay, 1984. Marie Elliott photos.

The Queen of the Islands.

The Sechelt Queen. *Photos courtesy B. C. Ferry Corporation.*

5

THE TIDES OF CHANGE: 1960-1980

From 1960 onwards the outer Gulf Islands were caught up in a number of movements that greatly affected their future development and the comfortable existence they had enjoyed with the mainland and Vancouver Island. The steady growth in population of Victoria and Vancouver meant that the Islands were being rapidly drawn into the urban shadows of both cities. This integration was facilitated by improved highways, and, especially, the new British Columbia ferry system, which could transport large numbers of passengers and cars efficiently and rapidly to any part of the Georgia Strait region. At the same time, rising incomes, increased leisure time, and a "back to the country" movement created a demand for vacation and retirement homes within easy commuting distance of British Columbia's two largest metropolitan areas.

As municipalities, towns and villages grew rapidly during this time period, and spread into unorganized territory, the provincial government became increasingly concerned about the uncontrolled settlement patterns. Lack of zoning regulations and a growing awareness of environmental and social problems led to major government intervention into land use planning for the entire province. Similar action was occurring elsewhere in North America as society became convinced that the government should take a more active part in promoting economic and social welfare.[1] All these social and political changes touched the Gulf Islands in the two decades between 1960 and 1980.

A noticeable retreat from the city began in the United States between 1940 and 1950 when the rural non-farm population became larger than the rural farm population. By 1960 five out of six country residents were non-farmers. In Canada the retreat to the countryside came a few years later. Although the rural population remained stable beetween 1951 and 1976, the percentage of non-farmers grew from 48% to almost 77%, or three out of four people.[2]

During this same time period, between 1951 and 1971 the population of greater Vancouver and greater Victoria doubled.[3] The combined population of the Capital Regional District and the Greater Vancouver Regional District represented two-thirds of British Columbia's total population in 1971. Increased wages, flexible working hours, and the implementation of better transportation facilities then allowed mainland

and Vancouver Island middle class families to seek vacation and retirement property close to home. With a rising cost of living, real estate investment in low-taxed, inexpensive island property seemed an excellent hedge against inflation.[4]

The Gulf Islands became easily accessible to the mainland when the provincial government inaugurated the long-awaited ferry link between Tsawwassen and Salt Spring Island on July 3, 1963, just in time for summer traffic. The new ferry, *Queen of the Islands,* could accommodate forty cars and four hundred passengers, and called at Galiano, Mayne and a new terminal at Long Harbour on Salt Spring, making two return trips daily to Tsawwassen. North Pender and Saturna were connected by feeder service, employing the *Motor Princess,* to Village Bay, but eventually North Pender was also made a port of call for the new ferry.[5]

It came as no surprise to some long-time residents that the new ferry rapidly became outmoded. Salt Spring Island travellers, who once preferred the Fulford Harbour-Swartz Bay-Tsawwassen route to the mainland, now created overflow situations most summer weekends by boarding at Long Harbour, leaving little space for Galiano, Mayne and Pender commuters.[6] A reserve booking system was implemented, which continues to this day, even though the *Queen of the Islands* was replaced by the larger *Sechelt Queen* in 1968, by the *Queen of Sidney* in 1976, and by the *Queen of Tsawwassen* in 1983.[7]

With daily service by the *Motor Princess* (renamed the *Pender Queen* and replaced by the *Mayne Queen* in 1965) from Swartz Bay, the residents of Mayne and the outer Gulf Islands were satisfied once again with transportation facilities, but easier access brought land speculators and soon more subdivisions were being slashed into a number of large property holdings, especially on Mayne and North Pender Islands. Magic Lake Estates on North Pender was termed the single largest subdivision in the Capital Regional District in 1967, with 1,450 lots.[8] The air rang with the noise of hammers and saws as newcomers prepared summer cabins and retirement homes. Within a single decade, Mayne Island's resident population grew from 278 to 495, between 1966 and 1976. During the summer months visitors swelled this total to more than one thousand.[9]

Representatives of real estate companies on the mainland opened offices and took up residence on the Islands in order to be closer to the lucrative market. Twenty-five acre lots that sold for $18,000 in 1962 brought $40,000 in 1967. By 1969 waterfront lots of one-third to one-half an acre on Mayne Island were selling from $8,500 to $9,000, and semi-waterfront property of similar size commanded $3,795 to $4,850. Dalton Deacon's beautiful valley farm at Village Bay was subdivided, with only a small portion remaining as hobby farms, as investors were urged to take advantage of the "Gulf Islands' first 'undevelopment'," with 10% down and the remainder payable at 8% or 9% interest.[10]

In November 1969 Dr. C. S. Holling, director of the University of Biritsh Columbia's Institute of Animal Resource Ecology, announced some of the findings from a computerized study of the Gulf Islands. Funded by a $500,000 grant from the Ford Foundation, the study involved thirty graduate students and faculty members feeding information covering the previous 69 years of development into the computers, and formulating predictions for the next ten, twenty and thirty years. Based on land use

Village Bay and the Dalton Deacon farm before subdivision, ca. 1940. The large barn on the right is still in use today. Mabel Foster photo.

trends, the "appalling" predictions for 1980 were that "80 per cent of all the first class recreation land in the Gulf Islands would be intensively developed." Holling further predicted that by 1980 all the recreation land in the Gulf Islands would be in private hands unless something was done to arrest development. The day prior to the release of Holling's findings, the provincial government imposed a ten-acre land freeze on development in the Gulf Islands as a holding action to give the regional districts involved time to prepare zoning regulations. Holling felt that two years was "the absolute maximum time" that could be allowed to pass before "rigid land use policy" had to be implemented.[11]

The strong conservationist stance of the Holling report contrasted sharply with that of some real estate developers. One agent argued that the Gulf Islands should be heavily developed, leaving the Fraser Valley for agricultural purposes:

> The idea of anybody today standing out on 10 acres or better of an ideal recreational and retirement area and saying look here, I am not going to let anybody come in and develop my land — that's absolute baloney, bilge of the worst order, dog in the manger attitude number one.[12]

He predicted that Mayne Island's population could jump from 250 to 10,000 people in five years, and that the island could sustain 50,000 people. For North Pender Island he forecasted a population of 15,000 to 25,000.

In spite of its small size, Mayne Island was highly developed by 1978. Of its 1,387 lots, only one-third had been built upon. Advertising as far away as Alberta had attracted many speculators, but the stories of American investments in the larger Gulf Islands were later proven false. An Islands Trust study in 1978 revealed that American ownership amounted to only 1.5% of the total property on the thirteen major islands in the Trust, and that Mayne Island, where only 18 parcels of land were owned by United States citizens, represented the overall average.[13]

Until 1965 subdivisions were permitted on a fragmented basis in unorganized territory in British Columbia if the necessary road provisions were approved by the Department of Highways, and water supplies and septic tank fields were approved by the Department of Health. To cope with the rapid expansion of communities and metropolitan areas in British Columbia in the 1960's, a proliferation of local planning boards and hospital boards sprang up. These local groups jealously guarded their authority, but it was becoming increasingly clear to the provincial government that some form of over-all regional agency was needed to integrate these services and "speak for the region as a whole."[14] Adopting a low key approach, the provincial government passed legislation in 1965, establishing regional districts throughout the province. Their functions were not assigned but acquired according to the needs and resources of the area involved. By 1968 twenty-eight districts had been established, covering all but a small portion of northwestern British Columbia.[15] Salt Spring Island and the outer Gulf Islands, already organized into hospital and school districts, were included in the Capital Regional District, which also embraced the Saanich Peninsula, Oak Bay, Victoria, Esquimalt, View Royal, Colwood, Langford, Metchosin and Sooke. The

CRD was incorporated on February 1, 1966.[16]

The new regional level of government was directed by a regional board comprised of representatives from municipal and non-municipal areas. In the case of the CRD, the non-municipal area of the southern Gulf Islands was divided into two electoral districts, Salt Spring and the Outer Gulf Islands, with each district electing one regional director. Regional directors on the CRD Board had the same voting privileges as municipal directors who represented incorporated municipalities, but whereas the two regional directors from the Gulf Islands had one vote each, municipal directors had from one to five votes, each vote representing 5,000 people. For example, the three directors from Saanich had a combined vote of fifteen.[17]

The regional districts assumed new functions by "a vote of its member areas, at the suggestion of the provincial government, or by order of the Lieutenant-Governor in Council." At the same time it was also possible for rural areas to form improvement districts in order to raise money through local taxes and loans from the provincial government to finance water systems, fire protection and ambulance services.[18]

The most obvious drawbacks to the inclusions of the outer Gulf Islands and Salt Spring in the CRD were the distances of the Islands from CRD headquarters in Victoria, and the fact that the directors from the two island districts held only two votes out of a total of fifty-two, on a predominantly urban Board. Islands directors could easily be outvoted by urban members who had little knowledge of island problems. Further north in Georgia Strait, other island residents found themselves attached to either mainland or Vancouver Island regional districts, with each district offering different levels of service.[19]

As subdivisions proliferated in the Gulf Islands and in the western communities of the CRD without any zoning regulations, the provincial government introduced further legislation, giving the Minister of Municipal Affairs discretionary powers over the regional directors' responsibilities. Under the Local Services Act (RSBC 1960, C224) the Minister could act as mayor-in-council and received the power to impose land use plans. On October 31, 1969, this power was exercised when the Lieutenant-Governor in Council declared the Gulf Islands as far north as Cortez Island a "local area" under the Act, and prohibited subdivisions under ten acres. The provincial government allowed a cut-off date of March 31, 1970, to permit on-going subdivision plans to be finalized. Between November 1969 and March 1970 a total of 1,900 lots were applied for on Salt Spring and the outer Gulf Islands, compared with an average of only 374 lots per year in the previous three years. Elsewhere in the Capital Regional District, a twenty-square-mile area bounded by Finlayson Arm and William Head, to the west of Victoria, was also placed under the same 10-acre minimum restriction.[20]

Defending his actions, Minister for Municipal Affairs Dan Campbell stressed the need to protect the environmental and recreational potential of the Gulf Islands:

No one perhaps likes the implications involved in regulation, but we cannot on the one hand talk about open spaces and control of the pollution of the environment without having some regard as to the use of our existing open space. The high public recreational value of the Gulf Islands makes this even more apparent because it is unlikely that anyone would suggest that a totally urban environment is the best use of land in all of the Islands stretching from Victoria to Kelsey Bay.[21]

Without issuing any explicit instructions, Campbell expressed hope that the regional districts would come up with community plans that they could administer, but he also hinted that he could use his powers as mayor-in-council to impose land use plans should the districts not conform: "I believe that time is running out on these local authorities to get on with the job."[22] The outer Gulf Islands district was allowed to appoint five members plus a director to an Advisory Planning Commission, and the staff of the CRD provided technical assistance.[23]

On April 1, 1970, planning for the outer Gulf Islands and Salt Spring Island officially came under the jurisdiction of the CRD. More technical help, such as building inspectors, was transferred to the CRD offices, and by-laws were introduced, imposing national building and plumbing codes. Sewage disposal remained the responsibility of the Department of Health.[24] By this time the CRD was well aware that the Gulf Islands required urgent attention,[25] and the District immediately set to work. Chairmen for the Salt Spring and Outer Gulf Islands Advisory Planning Commissions were chosen.[26]

In late 1971 the CRD attempted to gain local involvement in planning for the Islands when its planning department circulated 7,700 copies of a tabloid-style questionnaire entitled "Gulf Islands Options" to residents and commuters to the Islands, asking them to indicate their wishes for the future of the region. Respondents could choose from three options, or could design a fourth option of their own.[27]

Option A was the most extreme plan proposed by the planning department, and was included because P. A. Gaglardi had recently revealed that such a plan had been secretly prepared at his personal request, when he was Minister of Highways in 1967, by Tamco Engineering, Vancouver, at a cost of $80,000.[28] This option was a highway-bridge link connecting Swartz Bay to Salt Spring, Salt Spring to Galiano, Galiano to Mayne, and Mayne to Saturna. Ferries would then use only Galiano as the western terminus. (See map p. 101) Other alternatives within this option were more ferries instead of bridges to accommodate traffic, or a hydrofoil service (hovercraft). The questionnaire described this option as meeting all transportation demands in the most economical way. It was estimated that 20,000 to 25,000 part-time and permanent residents of the Islands would result. New towns on Salt Spring, Galiano and Mayne would accommodate the increased population. With rapid connections via ferry to the mainland, the Islands could easily become another suburb of Vancouver.[29]

Option B offered limited growth. Specified areas of settlement would be allowed to increase in population from 5,960 people in 1971 to a maximum of 23,930 in the future. Conservation areas, rural areas and forest land would be set aside to preserve the rural environment of the Islands. The CRD questionnaire posed two questions under this option: "Is it just a delaying action, temporarily diverting or retarding the march of urbanization? Does it mean that it will take thirty years to urbanize the Islands rather than fifteen?"[30]

Option C involved major park acquisitions, with the remainder of the land handled as in Option B. In 1971 the cost was estimated at $15 million to purchase 38 square

MAP No. 4

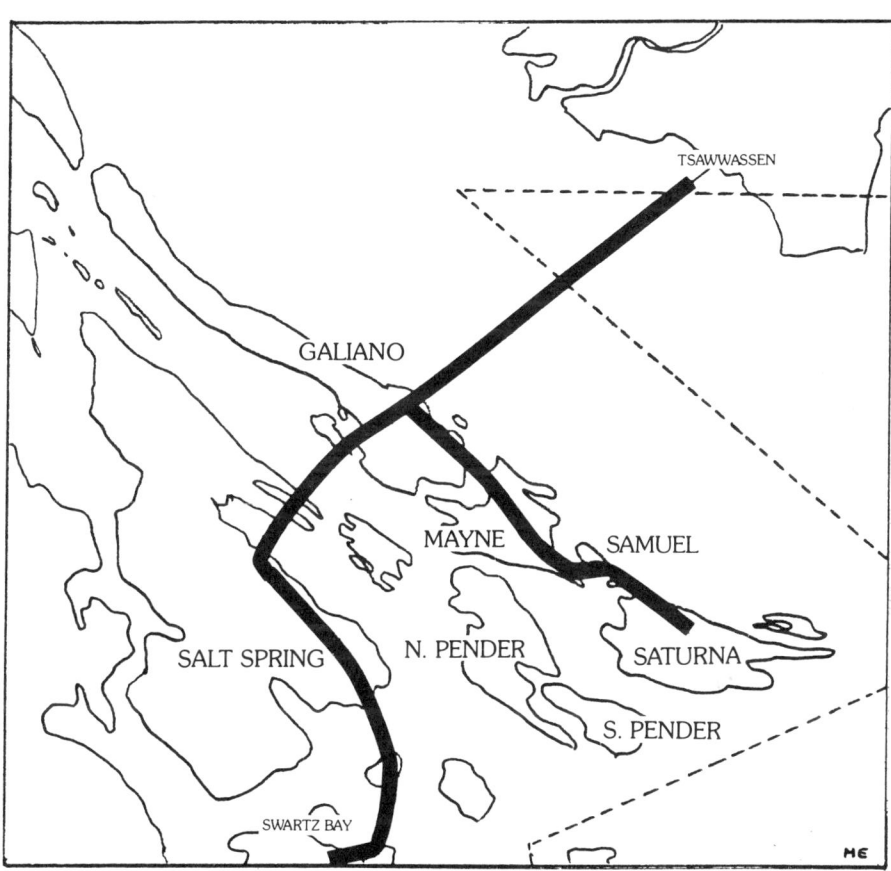

Bridge Proposal, "Gulf Islands Options," CRD
(based on map prepared by Capital Regional District, with permission)

miles of public land. Included would be the islands of Sidney, James, Brethour, Prevost, Parker, Secretary, Samuel and Curlew, plus land areas on all the main islands. To prevent over-crowding, ferry service would continue on a small scale, and provision for pedestrian access only would be made in order to cut down automobile use. The questionnaire explained that Option C was a matter of priorities, for $15 million could be spent by the provincial government to build a hospital, or to increase welfare payments. The land available for settlement on the Islands would be most expensive under this option, especially waterfront property.[31]

For Option D recipients of the questionnaire were provided with a blank map of the Islands and requested to make up their own proposal. At the end of the questionnaire nine additional questions were asked related to all the options.[32]

It was obviously an excellent attempt to obtain grass roots involvement in future planning for the Gulf Islands, but the CRD received a disappointing response rate of only 8%, or 577 completed questionnaires. Of these, 207 were from Gulf Island residents, and therefore the majority were received from non-residents. Twenty residents and fifty non-residents (i.e., visitors) participated from Mayne Island. Despite the lack of enthusiasm, the CRD felt there was a sufficient response rate to represent public opinion, and they published a summary of their findings.[33]

The respondents had been very consistent in their wishes that the Islands be preserved as a rural area. Of all options, 203 preferred Option C and 182 Option B. In answer to Question 2, "Do you favor a bridge from Vancouver to Victoria?", 510 of the 577 replied in the negative. The new town concept in Option A was rejected by 424 respondents, while 365 favored major parks on the Islands — 194 thought the amount of land proposed was about right, but 108 felt it was not enough. Most of the Mayne Island participants wanted a population ceiling of 2,000 to 3,000, compared to Galiano's preference for 3,000 to 4,000; North and South Pender, 4,000 to 6,000; and Saturna, 1,500 to 2,000.[34]

An official regional plan for the Gulf Islands was completed towards the end of 1972 and given initial approval by the CRD. Under the plan the 10-acre freeze would continue "unless the subdivision occurs in an island which is regulated according to the provisions of an official community plan." Protection of the rural country environment was the chief aim. Preliminary zoning by-laws for Salt Spring Island and the outer Gulf Islands were enacted January 13, 1971, and June 27, 1972, respectively.[35]

In spite of the 10-acre freeze, the Islands continued to be threatened by large developments. MacMillan-Bloedel proposed to subdivide 900 acres of a Tree Farm on Galiano into 1,500 lots, and a 550 lot subdivision on Gabriola was cancelled after residents appealed to Dan Campbell.[36] Because of the publicity concerning this latter case, Campbell agreed to set up an investigating committee to look into land development on the Gulf Islands. This proposal was inherited by the new NDP provincial government elected in August 1972, which formed a committee on municipal matters, chaired by Alf Nunweiler, MLA for Fort George, and composed of eleven MLAs, including the Minister of Municipal Affairs and representatives from all four political parties. The committee's task was to "inquire into the question of the future development of the Islands." The existing sections of the Municipal Act and other acts affecting local government were to be reviewed as part of the process, with a view to making recommendations. The committee also encouraged representatives from the various regional districts to make presentations, inasmuch as all the Islands north to Denman and Hornby were included in the inquiry.[37] They then toured the Islands in May and July 1973, holding public hearings that were generally well-attended by island residents. A special one-day visit was made to the University of British Columbia's Institute of Animal Resource Ecology, where Dr. Holling arranged a computer presentation related to his 1969 Gulf Island study.[38]

In a report to the provincial legislature, September 21, 1973, the committee noted that large subdivisions and over-development were priority concerns. More supervised public space was required, and water transportation would be the key factor in determining the extent of development, with control and coordination the responsibility of the provincial government rather than the region. They further observed that coordination between provincial departments, and between the regional districts and the province was seriously lacking. Recreation, moderate residential use and preservation of the rural atmosphere would be the priorities for land use. The committee ended their investigation with four recommendations:

1. Regional district boundaries should be reviewed and adjusted to assure that the Islands were in the most appropriate district. (This applied more to the northern Islands such as Hornby and Denman.)
2. An Islands Trust should be established. The committee emphasized that the Trust "must not be a separate and/or remote agency, but rather a fully representative coordinating body whose task it is to bring together each group, agency or department of government and to act in the best interests of the Islands and their residents, with due regard for the broader and province-wide interest."
3. No subdivisions should be permitted until a Trust is established.
4. The ten-acre freeze should continue on the northern Islands.[39]

The idea of a separate regional district for the Gulf Islands was considered and discarded as not being practical for a number of reasons, especially because available powers would be limited as outlined in the Municipal Act, and the regional tax base would be inadequate.[40]

Hugh Curtis, MLA for Saanich and the Islands, urged the government to act on the completed report, claiming that "the Islands have been left in limbo since 1969."[41] The Islands Trust concept was the unique aspect of the report because there were few Trust areas in North America to use as models.[42] As a consequence, the Trust would suffer many birth pains, including a lengthy test case in court, before receiving recognition and cooperation from provincial government departments who jealously guarded their authority.

While an Islands Trust was being established, the Advisory Planning Commission for the outer Gulf Islands continued to work on community plans and zoning regulations. South Pender and Galiano Islands adopted their community plans in January 1974, but North Pender and Mayne Island required more time, not gaining full community approval until 1976 and 1978 respectively. Both Saturna and Mayne concentrated their initial efforts on implementing zoning by-laws — most crucial in Mayne Island's case — and these were put in force in June 1972. Subdivision by-laws came later for most of the Islands: South Pender and Saturna in 1977, North Pender and Galiano in 1978, and Mayne not until 1981.[43]

The Islands Trust Act was introduced in the legislature on April 24, 1974, and given final approval June 5, 1974. The object of the Trust was to "preserve and protect, in cooperation with municipalities and the government of the province, the trust area and its unique amenities and environment for the benefit of the residents of the trust area and of the province generally." The Trust consisted of three government appointed general trustees and two locally elected trustees from each of the thirteen islands involved: Bowen, Denman, Gabriola, Galiano, Gambier, Hornby, Lasqueti, Mayne, North Pender, Salt Spring, Saturna, South Pender and Thetis, making 29 trustees in all. The trustees were empowered to:

> ... make recommendations to the cabinet on general development policy for the Islands, make recommendations to the cabinet on the acquisition and use of Crown Land in the area, coordinate and assist in the determination, implementation and carrying out of municipal and provincial government policies for the Islands, and make decisions on specific developments or zoning by-laws.[44]

The Trust would have veto power over any by-law passed by the regional district affecting the development of the Islands, including zoning, community development plans and subdivisions. Municipal Affairs Minister James Lorimer stated that "the Islands have just been kind of a dump on the regional districts," and that provision for local trustees would give the Islands better representation.[45]

One negative factor in the Trust proposal was the provision that appeals could be made only to the Minister of Municipal Affairs and not to the courts. Hugh Curtis was critical of this condition as well as the ratio of three appointed and two elected trustees on each Island committee: "It would be better to have three local trustees and two government appointed ones."[46]

Jim Campbell of Saturna, regional director for the outer Gulf Islands and chairman of the CRD, also criticized the trustee arrangement. He strongly opposed the concept "that would introduce appointed people to second-guess elected people."[47] The criticism from Campbell and Curtis was mollified somewhat when Hornby Island resident Hilary Brown was appointed chairman, and Marc Holmes of Salt Spring, vice-chairman. David Brousson, former Liberal MLA from North Vancouver, was the third general trustee.[48]

Local criticism of the Islands Trust came from residents who had managed to help organize water and hospital districts without the government's help and, therefore, did not feel it was necessary to have help with land planning.[49] When Hugh Curtis visited Mayne Island, the residents explained that they simply distrusted the imposition of another level of government, not knowing what the future would bring.[50]

The provincial government had done its best to involve local people in the formulation, implementation and administration of the new Island Trust policies, but the cooperation between the Trust and the CRD between 1974 and 1977 was not always harmonious. The CRD did not like the fact that the Trust had a veto power over plans and by-laws that could require many months of planning, yet the Trust could not implement land use plans of its own. Furthermore, the imbalance of representation on the Local Trust Committees of three apppointed general trustees and two elected local trustees continued to be a sore point.

In the spring of 1977 amendments to the Islands Trust were introduced in Bill 25 to take away control of planning and land use from the regional districts and give them to the Trust. Hugh Curtis, by now Minister for Municipal Affairs under the reinstated Social Credit government, claimed that the Bill would permit "greater responsiveness to local factors and would smooth a cumbersome approval process."[51] He was immediately accused of not consulting with the regional districts before introducing this Bill, and its passage was delayed until August 31, 1977, while the regional directors involved presented their suggestions to him and to Premier W. Bennett. Their criticism, plus that of the three opposition parties led to a further amendment that provided for the three general trustees to be elected rather than appointed. A further refinement in 1978 allowed residents of the smaller islands in the Trust area to vote in trustee elections, too.[52]

At the present time the Local Trust Committees are responsible for local planning, e.g., zoning, community plans and local policy, on the thirteen designated island groups (some small islands are included with each of the thirteen large islands). The General Trust Committee, which is made up of the three general trustees elected from among the twenty-six local trustees, is responsible for local planning on three hundred or more non-designated small islands, and for general problems and land use planning that affect two or more designated island groups.[53]

Five-member Advisory Planning Commissions for each of the designated island groups provide grass roots input, but their recommendations may be overruled by the Local Trust Committees.

* * * * *

A major test case for the validity of the Islands Trust commenced on Mayne Island in 1977, and was not resolved by the provincial Supreme Court until November 1981. If the final judgement had been found against Islands Trust, local residents believed that it would have amounted to the Trust's "death knell," and left the Gulf Islands wide open for exploitation.[54] The case involved Pinchin Holdings Ltd., owners of the Mayne Inn at Bennett Bay, and the company's attempt to build a large, commercial dock on the foreshore zoned for private use, adjacent to one of the best bathing beaches on the island.

Because the foreshore was considered Crown Land, Pinchin Holdings applied to the Land Management Branch for a foreshore lease in 1976 with the intention of operating a marina. After consulting Islands Trust, the CRD, and concerned provincial and

The disputed wharf at Bennett Bay in August 1979. Marie Elliott photo.

federal authorities, the Land Management Branch issued a letter of allowance — in effect a conditional approval for a lease — in September 1977. The letter stated that Pinchin Holdings must obtain re-zoning from private to commercial foreshore, as recommended by the CRD and Islands Trust. However, before applying for re-zoning, they installed twenty-one pilings in March or April 1978, extending one hundred meters out from shore. The Land Mangement Branch responded by issuing a "stop-work" order.[55] Residents of the Bennett Bay area had never been consulted by the CRD or Islands Trust regarding the marina, and visitors to the swimming beach that summer were given a taste of what might lie ahead. Numerous boaters, unable to tie up at the small float Pinchin Holdings had provided, anchored and sometimes even beached their crafts in close proximity to bathers. Noise and garbage pollution were further detriments.

During the next four years Pinchin Holdings pressed for the completion of their dock, while opposition grew. The Bennett Bay Preservation Committee consisted of 250 members and had many sympathizers. At a lengthy re-zoning hearing in April 1979 the Trust read 201 submissions and heard twenty-seven verbal submissions, with the majority against building the dock. The Mayne Island Trust Committee therefore decided not to give further readings to the re-zoning by-law.[56]

By this time half of the $50-60,000 project had already been completed, and Pinchin Holdings threatened to take their case to the Supreme Court if necessary.[57] When pile drivers returned to Bennett Bay in August 1979, Islands Trust immediately applied to the B. C. Supreme Court for an interim injunction to halt work and begin demolition.

The case was held before Mr. Justice J. G. Ruttan August 31, 1979, who granted the injunction pending trial of the action.[58]

The trial, scheduled for November 1979, was not heard until May 1980, when Mr. Justice F. C. Munroe declined to stop work, but held that the wharf must be kept for private use only. Islands Trust appealed in 1981, and won. Mr. Justice Seaton found that, although the dock was private, it was attached to a commercial land zone:

> I am satisfied that a dock serving a commerical enterprise situated on a contiguous lot is part of that commercial enterprise and further, that its use for access by guests and other persons visiting or having business with the respondent is not a use for private access.[59]

The fight against the Bennett Bay dock was a long and sometimes bitter ordeal for the concerned residents of Mayne Island, and for the Trust. It illustrates all to clearly that the ultimate strength of the Trust lies in its cooperation with many government agencies, and in the active participation of Gulf Islands residents. If the Bennett Bay Preservation Committee had not been so well organized, or if Pinchin Holdings had commenced their project a few years prior to 1977 when responsibility for local planning was transferred to Local Trust Committees, the decision on the dock might have been in their favor.[60]

* * * * *

The first half of this chapter has discussed the implementation of regional districts in British Columbia, the need for the Islands Trust, and the evolution of the Trust since 1974. There are limitations to the Trust's authority, however, and continuing pressures will be placed on the social and physical environment of the Gulf Islands by the burgeoning population of southwestern British Columbia. These pressures will necessitate changes to community plans, and possibly to the structure of the Trust itself. The last half of this chapter will discuss these limitations and pressures, and will conclude with a description of the social development on Mayne Island since 1960.

In most regional districts in British Columbia there are overlapping areas of authority among the various agencies responsible for local government. Crown corporations such as B. C. Hydro and B. C. Ferries, and provincial and federal ministries administering Agricultural Land Reserves, Crown lease applications, roads and highways, and Indian reservations have superior authority to local governments, including the Islands Trust. The Islands Trust Act empowers trustees to "coordinate and assist in the determination, implementation, and carrying out of muncipal and provincial government policies for the Islands," and "to make recommendations to the cabinet on the acquisition and use of Crown Land in the area." These responsibilities are not always recognized by outside agencies, however. The issuing of mining permits on Crown Land in the Trust area, and the establishment of a new ferry terminal, are recent examples of conflicting responsibilities.

108

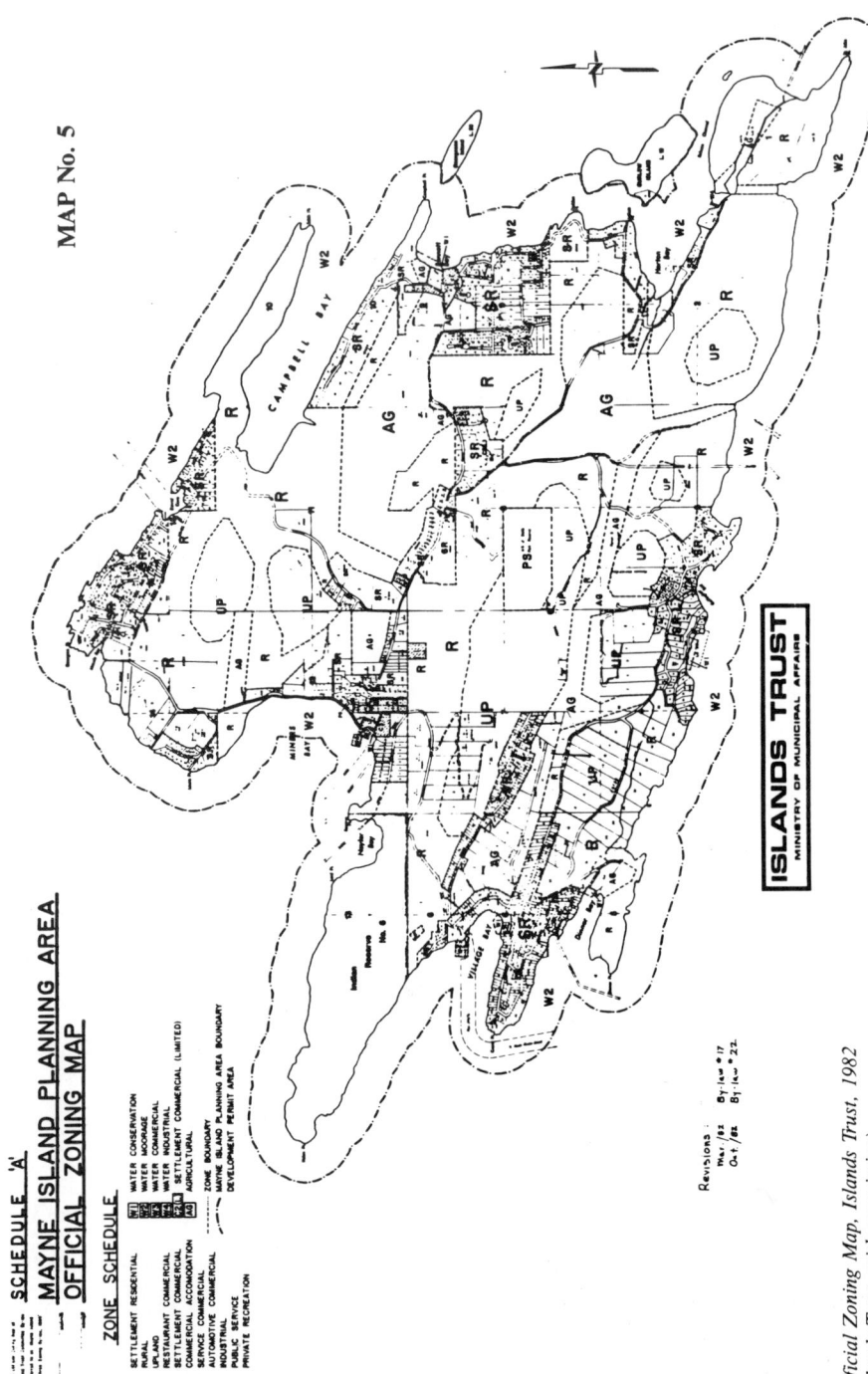

Official Zoning Map, Islands Trust, 1982
(Islands Trust, with permission)

Twenty per cent of the land area in the Trust is Crown Land. The small Crown Land reserve of eighty-four acres on Mayne Island will not likely be utilized in the near future, but residents of Gambier Island in Howe Sound are concerned about the possibility that an open pit copper mine may be built there by 20th Century Energy Corporation of Vancouver. Preliminary staking has covered 12,000 acres, including Crown Land. Permission to develop the mine on Crown Land may be given by the Ministry of Energy, Mines and Petroleum Resources, despite protests from the Gambier Island Local Trust Committee and from the General Trust Committee.[61]

The second area of conflict involves ferry transportation supplied to the Gulf Islands by the B. C. Ferry Corporation and the Ministry of Highways. In 1973 the all-party committee investigating land development on the Gulf Islands noted in its report to the legislature that water transportation would be the key factor in determining the extent of land development. A strong liaison needs to be maintained between the Islands Trust, the Ferry Corporation and the Ministry of Highways, but in the past this communication has sometimes been marginal. The plan for the Gabriola Island ferry terminal, for example, was reviewed behind closed doors before being placed in abeyance.[62]

In addition to the foregoing limitations of Trust authority, there are two other major areas of concern: the pollution of Georgia Strait, and the inability of the Trust to receive or administer gifts of land and money through an Islands Trust Fund.

Eighty-seven per cent of the Trust region is water, and as the number of pleasure craft in Georgia Strait proliferates each year, the question of how to control marine pollution becomes crucial. Sewage contamination from pleasure craft has already forced a number of shellfish closures during the summer months at various marine locations amongst the Islands. The difficulty lies in coordinating numerous levels of government. No less than seventeen federal and nine provincial acts contain relevant legislation that is administered by such diverse government departments as the provincial Ministry of Health, and the federal Environmental Protection Service and the Ministry of Fisheries and Oceans.[63]

Equally frustrating is the lack of an Islands Trust Fund. Section 3 of the Islands Trust Act provides for the establishment of such a fund, but to date the govenment has refused to proclaim this section. The Trust is therefore unable to accept gifts of land or money, and has no other means to acquire valuable natural or recreational areas, such as those recommended by the Nature Conservancy study conducted in cooperation with the Trust in 1975.[64]

* * * * *

The land and water resources of Mayne Island seem to be adequate for the population at the present time, but pressure will grow for more facilities as the development of the island increases.

Land use on Mayne Island is regulated by the community plan. Mayne Island's plan defines zoning for settlement, rural, upland, commercial, industrial, public service, water, recreation and agricultural areas, each specifying densities and permitted usage. (See map p. 108) Existing subdivisions, commerical operations and the Agricultural Land Reserve were taken into account when the plan was formulated, which meant that the project was very time-consuming. The present arrangement protects upland forested areas from high density development, thereby providing green belts to balance the more intensively subdivided valleys. Since the ten-acres freeze in 1969 very few large subdivisions have been approved. There are still more than 800 vacant lots on the island, and the potential exists for 215 more lots under the current zoning regulations. Given a population density of 2.5 people per lot, the eventual number of people living on Mayne Island, without any changes to the plan, could be 4,000.[65]

The watersheds of the Coast Range provide a reliable supply of fresh water for the resident of the lower mainland, and early settlers on Mayne and the outer Gulf Islands believed that their water came underground from Mount Baker, located one hundred miles to the east in the Cascade Range. Present day residents of the Gulf Islands would like to believe this myth, too, because the most fragile physical resource is potable water. To protect present and future demands, the regional Health Service imposes strict regulations on the Islands regarding water supply systems and sewage disposal. Many of the subdivisions introduced on Mayne Island since 1969 have public water systems rather than private wells, but two recent incidents of water pollution, at Bennett Bay and Miners Bay, have made the residents very sensitive to the relationship between sewage disposal and water supply.[66]

Not only must future demands from the mainland population for recreational and residential development on Mayne Island be weighed carefully against the limited land and water resources of the island, but the wishes of the permanent residents must be considered, as well. At a general meeting of the Islands Trust on Mayne in 1982 residents stated that they did not want to act as caretakers of a "park" for outsiders. This defensive stance is related to the growing need for police protection on the Islands. For more than fifty years a small police detachment at Salt Spring was adequate to handle law infractions in the southern Gulf Island area, but in the past decade the RCMP have established a detachment on North Pender Island, and placed officers on Galiano and Mayne Island from May until September. Transient visitors are often responsible for acts of vandalism, and breaking and entering. In addition, officers must ride the Tsawwassen to Salt Spring ferry on long weekends to curb rowdyism.[67]

The provincial government agreed that the Trust area was unique when it created the Islands Trust in 1974, but legislation can be amended or rescinded. In a surprise move on July 23, 1982, William Vander Zalm, Minister of Municipal Affairs, introduced Bill 72, a revised Land Use Act (that replaced the controversial Bill 9, withdrawn twenty-four hours earlier in the legislature), which included a section abolishing the Islands Trust. No provisions were made for a new form of local government; responsibility for planning and administering development on the Islands was to revert to the various regional districts. Vander Zalm defended his action as part of the government's budget restraint program during a recession year: "The burden on the taxpayer of operating an extra level of government should be eliminated."[68]

Following a hastily-called meeting of the Islands Trust Council in Nanaimo on July

Gulf Islanders demonstrate against abolishing the Islands Trust in Victoria, July 29, 1982. Thomas Ovanin photos.

24, protest lobbies were organized by Gulf Islands residents. These protests took the form of letters and telephone calls to government offices, and demonstrations outside the legislature from July 26 to July 29, on which date the House recessed. Bill 72 died on the order paper.[69]

Since the provincial election in 1983, a new Minister of Municipal Affairs, Bill Ritchie, has acknowledged the need for continuation of the Islands Trust as a protection agency, but with reservations:

> I am aware of past controversies about the Islands Trust. At the same time I acknowledge the need for the Trust as an agency for the continuing protection of the unique character of the Gulf Islands. This does not mean that the Trust will be allowed to evolve as a distinct, full-fledged level of government, nor that it will necessarily be exempt from measures of restraint and increased efficiency. Similarly, by endorsing the continuation of the Trust, I am by no means endorsing a policy of absolutely freezing the status quo on the Islands. The planning process must be responsive to the need for reasonable levels of sensitive development.[70]

The demonstrations in July 1982 proved that once granted, local autonomy may be difficult to rescind. Some Gulf Island residents have suggested that a new regional district might replace the Trust, but the necessary tax base is still just as elusive today as it was in 1973, when the idea was first considered by the all-party committee that recommended formation of the Islands Trust. — At the present time land owners in the Trust area are contributing only one third of the administration costs of the Trust through a 1.5 mill tax levy.[71]

* * * * *

While the regional districts, and then the Islands Trust were being implemented, the influx of new residents to the Gulf Islands between 1960 and 1980 brought more changes to the social amenities on the Islands. With the cessation of boat and mail days, interest in the preservation of the rural culture provided another focus for socialization. Having shared the rigorous travelling experience on the *Lady Rose,* when any more than fifty people in the lounge constituted a crowd, and the long, round-about trips of the early 1960's, when the Gulf Island Navigation Company no longer provided a mainland link to the Gulf Islands, many newcomers willingly worked together for the improvement of community services. On Mayne Island they served as officers on the various committees of the Mayne Island Agricultural Society, Mayne Island Ratepayers Association, and on the Advisory Planning Commissions for the CRD and the Islands Trust. Long-time residents were also elected to these committees for they owned large pieces of property and would be most affected by an increase in regulations or taxes. This harmonious integration of new and old residents agrees with the evidence found in studies elsewhere in North America of the rural acceptance of exurbanites.[72]

In 1966 the Mayne Island Ratepayers Association had accumulated enough money

The Queen of Sidney at Village Bay. B. C. Ferry Corporation photo.

to purchase a fire truck from the Port Moody Fire Department and to build a fire hall. A volunteer fire brigade, with a paid fire chief, met for regular practices. Pender and Galiano had formed their own fire protection groups a few years earlier, and Saturna followed in 1979. Better fire protection resulted in reduced fire insurance premiums for local residents. The Ratepayers Association also assumed responsibility for obtaining a first aid station in 1965, which was soon followed by the purchase of an ambulance, manned by a volunteer crew.[73]

The need for better health care for the increased number of residents on the island led to the formation of a committee to initiate plans for a health centre in 1975. With the assistance of the provincial government, the new centre opened in 1976, and a resident doctor and visiting Public Health nurse now care for the health needs of the community.[74]

Other community and social groups were formed as the population could support them: the Silver Maynes senior citizens group, the Lions Club, Paint and Sketch Club, and bridge and crib clubs. In addition, the Mayne Island Agricultural Society (which had taken over from the Maple Leaf Community Club of earlier years) cared for the community hall, restored the old police lockup and converted it into a museum,[75] operated a thrift shop, and continued to sponsor the annual fall fair established in 1925.

Church bells were heard once again every Sunday morning at Miners Bay, for the island had enough people to support a visiting Anglican minister from Victoria. Even non-residents came to be married, or to have their children christened at the unique sandstone font in the picturesque church of St. Mary Magdalene.[76] Services for Roman Catholic and other Protestant dominations were also held frequently in the community hall, the church or private homes.

By 1980 the population of Mayne Island was dominated by middle-aged, semi-retired and retired residents, but a number of younger people found an adequate source of income on the island, too. There were still numerous vacant properties that could be rented for a small sum, and in the late 1960's these attracted the "hippy" element. The other young group of newcomers were middle-class families who wanted to raise their children in the country. The fathers in these families usually owned their own businesses on the mainland, or had employment that allowed them to spend more than a weekend at their island homes. Some members of this group became enthusiastically involved in the land planning processes for Mayne Island, reflecting the growing international awareness of environmental problems by the younger generation at that time.

Children from these young families swelled the school population until it was necessary to enlarge the facilities. From a basic one-room school in the 1950's, offering grades one to eight, the Mayne Island school now offers kindergarten to grade nine inclusive, with home economics and industrial arts as part of the curriculum. Students in grades seven, eight and nine commute from Galiano and Saturna daily to attend junior high school classes on Mayne, but senior high school students on all the outer Gulf Islands must either attend the high school at Salt Spring, or elsewhere on the mainland or Vancouver Island.

Many of the new residents, young and old, are gifted artistically. Their talents support five local craft and art galleries, as well as an annual Christmas "faire." Quiet,

In 1982 a second dock was added to the Village Bay terminal, permitting an efficient transfer of vehicles from one ferry to another. This is a typical Sunday evening scene. The Mayne Queen (l) is discharging automobiles and passengers for the Queen of Tsawwassen, which will take them to Tsawwassen.

secluded locations in natural surroundings provide the creative atmosphere for professional artists and writers as well.

Between 1976 and 1981 Mayne Island had the slowest population growth of all the islands in the Islands Trust area. Its rate was 15 per cent compared to the highest rate, on Bowen Island, of 91 per cent. The 1981 Statistics Canada Census recorded a population of 560 for Mayne, but some residents thought that this figure should have been higher. Certainly, the population more than doubles on holiday weekends and during the summer with visitors and newcomers developing their vacation/retirement properties.[77]

* * * * *

After almost a century of laissez-faire existence, the residents of the Gulf Islands gradually accepted government restrictions on their lives, beginning in the 1960's. Events during the last two decades proved the most threatening to Mayne Island's rural and marine environment. Local government control, employing the unique concept of the Islands Trust, required the cooperation of other provincial government departments, which was not readily given.

Concern for the environmental protection of the Islands is a cohesive force that is certain to remain in view of the population pressures from the lower mainland. The ready acceptance of newcomers, evident in the early 1960's, is gradually changing to a more guarded response. This attitude was underscored when Islands Trust adopted a "welcome without promotion" policy for for tourist publicity in its official policy statement.[78] There was little criticisms of the policy at the public meeting held on Mayne Island.

The rich architectural heritage of the Gulf Islands is exemplified by the William and Anderina Deacon farmhouse, built in 1899 for $300, and restored by Alan and Hazel Steward. Marie Elliott photo.

6

CONCLUSION

Local history can be compared to the inner growth rings of a tree. It forms a vital core that is outwardly linked to national and international society.[1] While historical events on the Pacific coast swirled about them, the residents of Mayne Island and the outer Gulf Islands created their small community under adverse conditions more than one hundred years ago. They have played a small but important role in the development of the province ever since, especially in the southern Georgia Strait region.

Paradoxically, strong self-reliance and neighbourly cooperation were essential attributes of the earliest island settlers. In an island microcosm, ex-gold miners of diverse nationalities and their descendants easily accepted later arrivals, the Japanese and British immigrants. The Islanders' rural life-style required them to adjust not only to the forests but also to the sea, and the latter has proven to be the most dominant aspect of their landscape, providing a link with outside civilization, an element of danger, and the means whereby the area could be eventually exploited. The growing population of the mainland regarded the Gulf Islands as a rural paradise even before 1900, but it did not constitute a threat to land resources of the islands until two world wars had passed and the mode of ferry transportation improved in the late 1950's.

The impact of the large metropolitan areas of Vancouver and Victoria on the Georgia Strait urban area is presently gaining more attention from geographers and land planners. In this regard, Mayne Island's historical role is important as an example of how one community dealt with its vulnerability. The island initially supplied the mainland requisites of vacation facilities and fuel without difficulty, but the overwhelming demands for leisure property in the 1960's required government control. The provincial government's unique solution, the Islands Trust, is a concept rarely employed in North America, and the residents of Mayne Island have played a decisive role in testing the Trust's viability. While it has not achieved complete jurisdiction over land use planning matters, the Trust remains the major force for environmental protection of the Islands.

This study questions a number of accepted social viewpoints in British Columbia history, but much more work needs to be done before comparative studies can be made. Indian women in post-gold rush society were treated with love and consideration on Mayne Island, just as the Japanese also found ready acceptance. In the 1930's the Japanese represented one-third of the island population, yet they were not feared or vilified there as they were on the lower mainland of British Columbia. In the past, British immigrants have been singled out as the ones who civilized British Columbia: ". . . 'what we were in England or Scotland' was burnished and made the most of."[1] An examination of Mayne Island's cosmopolitan society reveals that not only English and Scots, but Indians, Germans, Japanese and Portugese contributed to the development of the socio-economic structure, and many of their descendants helped maintain it when the British pensioned families arrived after 1900.

At the present time urban historians are making valuable studies of large metropolitan areas, but the small towns and rural communities that lie in the paths of these growing cities need to be considered, too, if we are to gain the greatest understanding of our past, and the necessary insights for dealing with the future. The problems of how best to preserve the finite land and water resources of the Gulf Islands will require increasing attention as the population of southwestern British Columbia continues to expand. In a moral context, the Islands can be seen as pieces of a larger puzzle: what rights do rural areas have in the face of urban demands for recreation and housing? The next twenty years will be a time of serious probing and compromise as the solutions to these problems are sought by residents of the Gulf Islands, members of the Islands Trust, and related provincial and federal ministries.

Jack Aitken's store at Miners Bay, ca. 1910. Jack Aitken photo.

Yesterday and today, heritage homes at Miners Bay.

Peter Garrick built this large home for his family in 1914. Photo courtesy of Margaret Bennett.

APPENDIX I

Voters' Lists for 1879, 1909 and 1949

LIST OF PERSONS ENTITLED TO VOTE*

in the

ELECTORAL DISTRICT OF COWICHAN

1879

Buckly, Noah	Pender Island	Farmer
Campbell, John C.	Mayne Island	Farmer
Clagshaw, Henry	Galiano Island	Farmer
Collinson, William T.	Mayne Island	Farmer
Elford, Theophilus	Saturna Island	Farmer
Elford, William	Saturna Island	Farmer
Flett, John	Mayne Island	Farmer
Groth, Charles	Pender Island	Labourer
Georgeson, Henry	Plumpers Pass	Fisherman
Heck, Jacob	Mayne Island	Farmer
Hope, David	Pender Island	Farmer
Hope, Rutherford	Pender Island	Farmer
Morris, Henry	Galiano Island	Farmer
Puetz, John	Mayne Island	Farmer
Robson, Frederick	Mayne Island	Farmer
Silva, John	Mayne Island	Farmer
Sutherland, Daniel	Samuel Island	Farmer
Trueworthy, Charles	Saturna Island	Farmer
Tatton, Isaac	Tumbo Island	Farmer
Weston, William	Mayne Island	Farmer
Wick, John	Mayne Island	Farmer

*The Cowichan electoral district also included Shawnigan, Quamichan, Chemainus, Comiaken and Somenos.

LIST OF PERSONS ENTITLED TO VOTE*

in the

THE ISLAND ELECTORAL DISTRICT

November 1st, 1909

Adams, James	Pender Island	Missionary
Adams, Herbert Thompson	Pender Island	Farmer
Aitken, John	Galiano Island	Farmer
Ainslie, Gilbert Hamilton	Pender Island	Farmer
Aldridge, Augustus Henry	South Pender	Farmer
Allison, Frank Togan	Porlier P., Galiano	Lighthouse keeper
Andrews, Samuel Clarke	North Pender	Farmer
Andrew, Henry	North Pender	Farmer
Auchterlonie, Lawrence	Pender Island	Farmer
Auchterlonie, James	Pender Island	Farmer
Beale, Holden Leroy	Galiano Island	Farmer
Beale, Walter A.	Galiano Island	Farmer
Bennett, David	Mayne Island	Farmer
Bennett, Thomas, Jr.	Mayne Island	Farmer
Bennett, Thomas	Mayne Island	Farmer
Bennett, James William	Mayne Island	Farmer
Bennett, John Alexander	Mayne Island	Farmer
Bennett, Frederick	Mayne Island	Farmer
Bellhouse, John Wortley	Galiano Island	Farmer
Bishop, Hubert	Pender Island	Farmer
Blake, William Henry J.	Mayne Island	None given
Blantern, John Wesley	Saturna Island	Farmer
Boyce, H. E.	Pender Island	Farmer
Brackett, James Alexander	Pender Island	Rancher
Burnette, Charles William	Mayne Island	Mariner
Burrill, Joseph	Galiano Island	Farmer
Burrill, Frederick James	Galiano Island	Farmer
Burnett, David Morrison	Galiano Island	Logger
Cayzer, Thomas Rolo	Galiano Island	Farmer
Cayzer, Alfred	Galiano Island	Farmer
Cain, William	Galiano Island	None given
Chivers, Jeremiah	Galiano Island	Farmer
Cook, John	Galiano Island	Farmer
Collinson, Melville	Mayne Island	Seaman
Collinson, William Tompkins	Mayne Island	Post Office
Colston, Robert C.	Pender Island	Farmer
Colston, Sweaney Basil	Pender Island	Farmer
Copeland, George	Pender Island	Farmer
Corbett, Robert Stewart W.	Pender Island	Farmer
Covil, Robert Percy	Mayne Island	Electrical engineer
Craig, Alexander	Galiano Island	Farmer
Cruickshank, William	Galiano Island	None given

Cullison, Judson A.	Galiano Island	None given
Darcey, Charles	Mayne Island	None given
Dakers, James Alexander	Saturna Island	Labourer
David, Francis Louis	Mayne Island	Farmer
Davidson, Andrew August	Pender Island	Farmer
Davey, Henry Thomas	Mayne Island	Farmer
Dean, Edwin Hugh Morris	Mayne Island	Marine engineer
Deacon, John	Mayne Island	Farmer
Deacon, William	Mayne Island	Farmer
Deacon, Dalton	Mayne Island	Farmer
Deacon, Andrew	Mayne Island	Farmer
Dickson, Archibald Francis	Mayne Island	Farmer
Dyne, George Bradley	Saturna Island	Farmer
Ekholm, John	Mayne Island	Farmer
Enke, Max	Galiano Island	Farmer
Fleming, William	Mayne Island	Farmer
Foot, Clarence	Galiano Island	Farmer
Gardom, Alfred Harold	Galiano Island	Farmer
Garrett, George Septimus	Pender Island	Rancher
Garrett, Percy Wallis	Pender Island	Rancher
Garrett, Peter	Pender Island	Netman
Georgeson, James	Saturna Island	Lighthouse keeper
Georgeson, George	Mayne Island	Farmer
Georgeson, Edward	Galiano Island	Labourer
Georgeson, Henry	Mayne Island	Lighthouse keeper
Georgeson, Andrew	Saturna Island	Boat builder
Gillespie, William Jardine	Mayne Island	Contractor
Goldie, Frank	Mayne Island	None given
Grey, Ralph Geoffrey	Samuel Island	Farmer
Grimmer, Washington	Pender Island	Farmer
Groth, John Henry	Galiano Island	Farmer
Hamilton, Alexander	Pender Island	Farmer
Harriss, George Stanley	Pender Island	Farmer
Hamilton, Hugh	Pender Island	Farmer
Harris, Howard B.	Pender Island	Farmer
Heneage, Charles E. F.	Saturna Island	Farmer
Heck, James Oscar	Mayne Island	Farmer
Heck, Frank Jacob	Mayne Island	Farmer
Heck, Jacob	Mayne Island	Farmer
Higgs, Lewis L. S.	South Pender	Farmer
Hooson, Evan	Pender Island	Farmer
Hoger, Henry	Mayne Island	Fisherman
Hope, Rutherford	Pender Island	Farmer
Hoffman, Peter	Pender Island	Labourer
Inglis, Archibald	Mayne Island	Farmer
Irwine, Edward	Galiano Island	Gentleman
Jack, Robert	Mayne Island	Farmer
Jack, Matthew James	Mayne Island	Farmer
MacKinnon, John	Pender Island	Farmer
Maude, Eustace D.	Mayne Island	Storekeeper
McDonald, Charles Jeremiah	Mayne Island	Hotelkeeper
McCoskrie, William	Galiano Island	Marine engineer
Menzies, Victor William	Pender Island	Farmer
Menzies, Albert Hugh	Pender Island	Farmer
Murcheson, Finlay Alex.	Galiano Island	Farmer
Murcheson, Finlay	Galiano Island	Farmer
Millington, William	Mayne Island	Bricklayer
Nicholson, Albert	Mayne Island	Farmer
Ouellette, Hector	Galiano Island	Fisherman

Paddon, George Locke	Mayne Island	None given
Paddon, John Locke	Mayne Island	None given
Paddon, William F. Locke	Mayne Island	Clerk in Holy Orders
Payne, Gerald Fitzroy	Saturna Island	None given
Payne, Harold Digby	Saturna Island	Farmer
Page, Stanley	Galiano Island	Farmer
Page, Joseph	Galiano Island	Postmaster
Percival, Spencer	Pender Island	Farmer
Pollard, Elijah	Pender Island	Rancher
Purden, Harold Wyatt	Pender Island	Rancher
Rae, Thomas Couston	Galiano Island	Farmer
Roe, Robert	Pender Island	Machinist
Roe, George	Pender Island	Farmer
Roe, Samuel Robinson	Mayne Island	Teacher
Robson, James	Mayne Island	Painter
Robson, Stanley Howard	Mayne Island	Farmer
Robson, James John	Mayne Island	Farmer
Robson, Frederick James	Mayne Island	Farmer
Robson, William Matthew	Mayne Island	Hotelkeeper
Russell, Edwin Andrew	Mayne Island	Farmer
Shields, Richard	Galiano Island	Farmer
Spalding, Arthur Reed	South Pender	Farmer
Spence, Clyde	Galiano Island	Rancher
Sturdy, Frederick	Galiano Island	Florist
Steward, Philip Arthur	Galiano Island	Farmer
Stanford, Arthur Edward	South Pender	Farmer
Shaw, John	Galiano Island	Farmer
Taylor, George G.	Saturna Island	Quarryman
Tinkley, John William	Mayne Island	Farmer
Vollmers, Harry	Galiano Island	Boat builder
Walker, William Tyrrel	South Pender	Farmer
Walker, John Matthew	Galiano Island	Farmer
Watson, George Andrew	Mayne Island	Fisherman
Warnock, James	Galiano Island	Farmer
Willey, John	Pender Island	Farmer
Winstanley, Oliver Tinson	Galiano Island	Farmer
Winstanley, Ernest Edward	Galiano Island	Farmer
Winstanley, Edw. Geo.	Galiano Island	Farmer
Worge, Charles Drummond	Galiano Island	Farmer
Wrigley, Robert A.	Galiano Island	Fisherman

*The Islands electoral district included North Saanich and Salt Spring, but only residents of the outer Gulf Islands have been selected for this list.

VOTERS LIST

NANAIMO AND THE ISLANDS DISTRICT

Polling Division No. 14 (Mayne Island)

May, 1949

Aitken, Fanny, housewife
Aitken, Grace, widow
Aitken, John, farmer
Aitken, John B., fisherman
Aitken, Mary Philip, housewife
Aitken, Robert, farmer
Aitken, Roy M., farmer
Angus, George, retired
Atterbury, James E., shipwright
Atterbury, Margaret J., housewife
Bardon, Harold R., retired
Bardon, Marjorie K., housewife
Barnes, Edwin, retired
Bennett, David, farmer
Bennett, Elsie, housewife
Bennett, Frederick, farmer
Bennett, Frederick J., horticulturalist
Bennett, John A., pensioner
Bennett, John H., farmer
Bennett, Lillian, spinster
Bennett, Margaret M., housewife
Bernard, David A., logger
Bernard, Helen E., housewife
Borthwick, G. Charles, logger
Bradshaw, Anne E., housewife
Bradshaw, John E., horticulturalist
Christie, Margaret H., housewife
Christie, Thomas D., retired
Cole, Charlotte M., widow
Colston, Sweany B., retired
Davis, Helen E., widow
Deacon, Alice M., housewife
Deacon, Anderina M., housewife
Deacon, Dalton, farmer
Deacon, Edith Mary, housewife
Deacon, Wilbert W., farmer
Dibley, Edith Amy, housewife
Dibley, George V., farmer
Farmer, Grace B., spinster
Fields, Elizabeth C., housewife
Forsyth, Muriel E., housewife

Forsyth, Owen S., resort owner
Foster, Mabel, widow
Foster, Mary Anne, housewife
Foster, Richard G., fisherman
Foster, Roland B., logger
Garrick, Kathleen, telephone operator
Garrick, Norah B., housewife
Garrick, Peter Leslie, lineman
Georgeson, Darrell, boat operator
Georgeson, Norman D., fisherman
Gilman, Betty E., housewife
Gilman, Geoffrey Beall, farmer
Gilman, Marguerite, housewife
Gilman, Reginald T., mine operator
Godkin, Doreen I., housewife
Godkins, Leonard Allan, logger
Greene, Walter M., retired
Gudmundson, Bertha A., housewife
Gudmundson, Eric, mill owner
Gunderson, Hans, fisherman
Gunderson, Petrine, housewife
Gurney, Hugh S., lighthouse keeper
Gurney, Kathleen, housewife
Haglund, Margaret, housewife
Haglund, Waldemar Davie, logger
Hall, Evelyn Nancy, telephone operator
Hall, Julia Mary, telephone operator
Hall, Nesta E., housewife
Hall, Richard, farmer
Hansen, Ferdinand, farmer
Hansen, Marvin E., logger
Heck, Frank, retired
Heck, Frederick L., retired
Hickman, Ada, cook
Higginbottom, Florence, housewife
Higginbottom, Walter P., carpenter
Horton, Alexander, fisherman
Horton, Doris, housewife
Hunt-Sowrey, Kathleen M., housewife
Hunt-Sowrey, Walter W., farmer
Jack, Henry, logger

Jackson, Alvin L., logger
Jackson Sylvia, housewife
Johnston, William, signal sender
Johnstone, Heather Yvonne, hairdresser
Jones, Anice Maude, widow
Juyn, Eugenie Cornelia, nurse
Kelso, Amelia, widow
Kirkland, Franklin, fisherman
Larson, Gottfrid, carpenter
Larson, Hans Carl, fisherman
Larson, Lydia May, housewife
Lewis, Jane Day, housewife
Littledale, Arthur R., retired
Littledale, Edward T., retired
Littledale, Gladys E., housewife
Lord, Jessie Duncan, housewife
Lord, John W. C., retired
Lord, Stuart Ross, student
Maiden, Annie E., housewife
Maiden, Fred, retired
Martin, Mary S., widow
Maynard, Elsie, housewife
Maynard, George H., retired
Morson, William H., horticulture
Morton, Frank Durfee, retired
Murphy William, farmer
Murrell, Constantia Edith, housewife
Murrell, Edward C., retired
McCann, Annie, widow
MacDonald, William D., pensioner
MacKay, Donald D., retired
Naylor, Emma, widow
Nechwediuk, Lynn, teacher
Neill, Elizabeth G., spinster
Neill, Janet A., spinster
Neill, John, retired
Norminton, Florence, housewife
Norminton, Frank, retired
O'Connor, Arthur James, farmer
O'Connor, May, housewife
Odberg, Bernhard G., blacksmith
Odberg, Edwin, logger
Odberg, Gordon, logger
Odberg, Mary Emily, housewife
Orman, Charles Frank, clergyman
Orman, Mabel Lily, housewife

Payne, Cecil A., retired
Payne, Mabel L., housewife
Pratt, Francis W., farmer
Pratt, Winnie M., housewife
Rashleigh, Donald S., retired
Rashleigh, Frances M., housewife
Revitt, Lizzie, housewife
Revitt, Walter C., retired
Roberts, Sophie L., housewife
Roberts, Thomas E., physician
Robson, Gordon Stanley, farmer
Robson, Mildred, housewife
Robson, Stanley Howard, farmer
Roulston, Jessica M., housewife
Roulston, Robert K., logger
Salmon, Elsie E., housewife
Salmon, Ethelwyn, housewife
Salmon, Richard A., merchant
Salmon, William H. merchant
Sheppard, Clifford L., logger
Sheppard, Lillian M., housewife
Smith, Herbert J., logger
Stallybrass, Bernard, fishbuyer
Stark, Helen Liddle, spinster
Steel, Alfred L., postmaster
Steele, Richard J., farmer
Steele, Eva, housewife
Taylor, Betty K., housewife
Taylor, Vincent C., retired
Underhill, Cecil Roe, retired
Underhill, Lucy E., spinster
Van-Welter, Emma, housewife
Van-Welter, Harley Loyd, fishbuyer
Vigurs, Arthur, retired
Vigurs, Donald J., farmer
Vigurs, Gertrude Mary, housewife
Viste, Johannes A., fisherman
Viste, Madeline L., housewfie
Waugh, James N. retired
Waugh, Kathleen M., housewife
Whiskin, Gwendoline A., widow
Wilks, Elsie May, housewife
Wilks, Pearl Christina, housewife
Wilks, Robert Baldwin, merchant
Wilks, William merchant
Worthington, Bessie R., housewife

APPENDIX II

Some of the Earliest Settlers

BENNETT, Thomas and Alice (nee Thom). A ship's carpenter by trade, Thomas and his family emigrated from Scotland about 1879 at the behest of an uncle, James C. Campbell, who had pre-empted property on the east side of Mayne (eventually called Bennett Bay) in 1876. Homesick and tired after the long journey by ship, and then by train across the United States, Alice took one look at her new homesite and deemed it "the arse end of the world." But with probably no training in farming, the family persevered and developed a large, prosperous farm. Five children emigrated with their parents: James, Annie, Thomas, Mary and John. Three more were born on Mayne: Frederick, David and Alice. Mrs. Bennett was well-known in the outer Gulf Islands as a midwife. She and her husband also operated the Point Comfort Hotel from 1896 to 1898.

COLLINSON, William Tompkins and Mary. Born near Northallerton, North Yorkshire, Tom emigrated to Canada West (Ontario) in 1850 with his family. In 1857 he left Ontario and headed west, via the United States, arriving in Whatcom County (Washington State) in time to hear the news of gold discoveries on the Fraser River in 1858. Tom took an active part in the developments that followed on the mainland, helping to build the Royal Engineer Road from New Westminster to Burrard Inlet. He initially pre-empted land near New Westminster, then later on Sumas Prairie. He also spent some time in the Cariboo, and is believed to have helped guide miners over the Seton Portage north of Harrison Lake. He and his Indian wife Mary moved to Mayne about 1871, and homesteaded on part of what is now the Robson farm. Two children, Melville and Elizabeth, were born at Sumas, and Emma, Margaret, Sam and James were born on Mayne.

COOK, Nicholas and Catherine (Kitty). Nicholas came from Germany and took part in the Fraser River gold rush in 1858. He registered his pre-emption of 100 acres on Mayne Island in 1864, which makes him one of the earliest settlers. There were three children: William, John and Carl. Cook died of natural causes in October 1870 at the age of 38. About 1872 Jacob Heck acquired Cook's property, and Catherine became Mrs. Heck.

DEACON, John and Margaret (nee Kirk). John was born at Innisfil township, Simcoe County, Upper Canada in 1834, and Margaret in Ireland in 1837. The family came west via the United States and San Francisco to New Westminster in 1880. They moved to Mayne Island soon afterwards, living first at Hardscrabble Farm, and then acquiring the farm of John and Louisa Silva at Village Bay. There were seven children: Dalton, William, Andrew, John, Frederick (who died in infancy), Caroline and Annie. In addition to operating a large farm, the Deacons converted their home into a summer boarding house about 1890, adding a second wing for guests in 1892. Margaret died in 1920 and John in 1922.

GEORGESON, Henry (Scotty) and Sophie (Caty). Henry was born in the Shetland Islands in 1835, and went to sea at an early age. He arrived in Victoria about 1856, and took part in the Cariboo gold rush, operating a stopping house at Beaver Pass, Lightning Creek, for several years. He moved to Galiano about 1863, but did not record his pre-emption there until 1873. Scotty earned his living by fishing for Alex Ewen's cannery, building boats, and serving as assistant keeper on the Sandheads lightship from 1880-1881. He became the first lighthouse keeper at Georgina Point lighthouse, Mayne Island in June 1885, and did not retire until December 31, 1920, at the age of 86. He received the Imperial Long Service Medal in October 1922, for 37 years of lighthouse service. Scotty died in 1927, and is buried in the cemetery he donated to the Galiano community. Sophie was born at Knacken Lake, British Columbia in 1829. She and Scotty had five children: Elizabeth, William, Henry, George and John.

GREAVY, James and Mary Jane. James was the son of William and Elizabeth Greavy of New Brunswick, and Mary Jane was born in Boston, Massachusets. William and Elizabeth Greavy, with sons William, and James with Mary Jane, emigrated to Oregon in the late 1850's or early 1860's, where William Sr. died. James may have been in partnership with Christian Mayers, operating a small ranch on Mayne Island, and likely was absent during the summer months working on Fraser River steamboats. He died at Soda Creek in September 1867. Mary Jane sold the property rights on Mayne Island to lawyer M. Tyrwhitt Drake of Victoria, who in turn sold them to William Collinson in 1881.

HECK, Jacob and Catherine. Jacob is believed to have been born in Prussia. Fresh from the Cariboo gold fields, Jacob and his friend John Puetz pre-empted adjoining property on Mayne Island in 1870. Jacob eventually owned 320 acres of prime valley property, and was a very successful farmer. In 1883 he donated the land for the first school. Jacob and Catherine had six children: Matilda, Alice, Dora, Frederick, Frank and James Oscar. Frank and Frederick served in World War I.

MAYERS, Christian and Mathilda. Christian Mayers was born in Plochingen, Kingdon of Wurttemberg (now south-western Germany). He and his Indian wife had three sons: George, Joseph and Frederick. Like his friend James Greavy, Mayers also worked on the river boats. He eventually relocated to New Westminster, where his son George became a well-known captain.

NICHOLSON, Alexander. There are many stories about this man, but the only fact we can verify is his early pre-emption, 1862, on part of the Hardscrabble Farm. His small holding is shown on Turner's 1874 survey map. When Nicholson died about 1875, he left behind the legend of buried gold on his property, which has tantalized residents and visitors ever since. He is believed to have taken part in the California, Australia and Cariboo gold rushes.

PUETZ, John. Puetz pre-empted 120 acres adjacent to Jacob Heck in 1870, but subsequently acquired 148 acres of property at Miners Bay in 1884. He built a small store and hotel on this site, near the government wharf. In addition to his farming and hotel careers, Puetz served as assessor and tax collector for the Cowichan district in 1878, and worked as an engineer on the Fraser River steamships in 1882. It appears that Puetz never married, and we cannot find any reference to him after 1888, when Warburton Pike acquired his Miners Bay property.

ROBSON, Frederick James. Even though he was fortunate to travel round the Horn to Victoria on the bride ship *Robert Lowe* in 1862, Frederick remained a bachelor all his life. He prospected in the Cariboo, attempted to homestead in the Fraser Valley, and then relocated to Mayne Island about 1871, where he farmed initially in partnership with William Collinson. Fred lived to be 89, and died in 1937.

ROBSON, William and Ann. William was born in Pimlico, London, in 1842, and Ann in 1847. This young family emigrated to New Zealand, and then to Mayne Island in 1879 to join William's uncle Frederick. Four children arrived with their parents: James, Eva, Emma and Annie who was born in New Zealand. Eliza and Stanley were born on Mayne. William and Ann operated Mayne Island House (John Puetz's hotel) for Warburton Pike, and for a subsequent owner, Archibald Inglis. The family then moved to Glenwood Farm and became well-known for their success with Jersey dairy herds. Like Alice Bennett, Ann was also known as an excellent midwife. William and Ann died in 1923, but Glenwood farm is still operated by members of the Robson family.

SILVA, John and Louisa. John emigrated as a sailor from the Azores, and arrived in Victoria about 1865. He operated a grocery store in Victoria for several years before pre-empting property at Village Bay, Mayne Island, in 1873. They had ten children, of whom John, Gabriel, Mary and Joseph were probably born at Mayne. About 1883 the family moved to Silva Bay, Gabriola Island.

NOTES

CHAPTER I

[1] Roger B. Stickney, "Sedimentology, Stratigraphy and Structure of the Late Cretaceous Rocks of Mayne and Samuel Islands, British Columbia" (M.Sc. thesis, Oregon State University, 1976), pp. 20-24; and Jory Allen Pacht, "Sedimentology and Petrology of the Late Cretaceous Nanaimo Group in the Nanaimo Basin, Washington and British Columbia: Implications for Late Cretaceous Tectonics" (Ph.D. dissertation, Ohio State University, 1980), pp. 3-6.

[2] Stickney, "Sedimentology," pp. 160-165.

[3] S. Eis and D. Craigdallie, *Gulf Islands of British Columbia* (Ottawa: Department of Supply and Services), p. 7.

[4] John T. Walbran, *British Columbia Coast Names* (Vancouver: J. J. Douglas Ltd., 1971), p. 11.

[5] Roy L. Carlson, "Excavations at Helen Point on Mayne Island," *B. C. Studies,* 6 and 7 (Fall and Winter, 1970), pp. 113-123; and James C. Haggarty and John H. W. Sendey, *Test Excavation at the Georgeson Bay Site, Gulf of Georgia Region, British Columbia* (Victoria: British Columbia Provincial Museum, 1976), p. 64.

[6] Henry R. Wagner, *Cartography of the Northwest Coast of America* (Amsterdam: N. Israel, 1968), p. 425; and Henry R. Wagner, *Spanish Exploration in the Strait of Juan de Fuca* (Santa Ana, California: Fine Arts Press, 1933), pp. 253-257. Punta de Anclage (i.e., anchorage) was probably the bay separating Gossip Island from Galiano, just north of Active Pass, since the rest of the Galiano coastline does not offer any protection from Georgia Strait until Porlier Pass is reached.

[7] "Haro Strait and Middle Channel," Map G786 har, 1872, Provincial Archives of British Columbia (hereafter cited as PABC).

[8] British Columbia, *Sessional Papers,* 1901, p. 591

[9] James Douglas, "Report of a Canoe Expedition Along the East Coast of Vancouver Island," *Journal of the Royal Geographical Society,* 24 (1854), pp. 245-248.

[10] Vancouver did not explore the Canadian Gulf Islands, but James Johnstone, Master of the *Chatham,* accompanied by botanist Archibald Menzies, may have done so. See *Menzies' Journal of Vancouver's Voyage* (Victoria: King's Printer, 1923), pp. 53-59.

Richard Charles Mayne, *Four Years in British Columbia and Vancouver Island* (London: John Murray, 1862; reprint ed. New York: Johnson Reprint Corporation, 1969), pp. 10 and 151.

[11] Mayne, *Four Years,* p. 207.

[12] Walbran, *B. C. Coast Names,* p. 11. The Hudson's Bay Company steamship *Beaver* used Porlier Pass at the north end of Galiano, rather than Active Pass, although the tidal bore could reach 7-8 knots in either waterway, and Porlier Pass had dangerous rocks in mid channel. Log of S.S. *Beaver* 1850-51, HBC Archives, C.1/208, fos. 9 and 55d, Provincial Archives of Manitoba; and George H. Richards, *Vancouver Island Pilot* (London: Hydrographic Office, Admiralty, 1864), p. 66.

[13] L. E. Sawyer, Manager, Public Affairs, British Columbia and Yukon Division, Canada Post, Vancouver, to author, November 9, 1979; British Columbia, *Sessional Papers,* 1896, p. 309; and *Victoria Daily Colonist,* November 2, 1900, p. 5, and October 10, 1909, p. 2 (hereafter cited as *Colonist).*

[14] The exact date of occupation is uncertain. When reporting the deaths of Frederick Marks and Caroline Harvey in 1863, Mayers indicated that he had lived at Miners Bay for two years. *Colonist,* April 10, 1863, p. 3.

[15] Probated will of Christian Mayers, 4755, and intestate papers of James Messenger Greavy, 296, folio 123, vol. 1, Central Probate Index, British Columbia Court Registry, Court House, Victoria.

[16] A. F. Fluke, "Early Days on Salt Spring Island," *British Columbia Historical Quarterly* 15-16 (July-October 1951), 165-166.

[17] *Colonist,* March 3, 5 and 12, 1867, all p. 3.

[18] Right Rev. George Hills, Journals, typescript, p. 21, British Columbia Provincial Synod Archives, Anglican Church of Canada, Vancouver (hereafter cited as Synod Archives).

[19] Charles Groth, Diary, passim., Add. MS 243, PABC; and interview with Frederick James Bennett, Mayne Island, November 1981. Fred Bennett is the grandson of pioneer resident Thomas Bennett.

[20] Mayne, *Four Years,* p. 19; and Will Dawson, *Coastal Cruising,* ref. 3d ed. (Vancouver: Mitchell Press, 1973), p. 22.

[21] *Colonist,* March 3, 1867, p. 3.

[22] Wilson Duff indicates a high concentration of Indians on southeastern Vancouver Island in a population distribution map for 1835, suggesting 3-4,000 natives. Wilson Duff, *The Impact of the White Man,* Anthropology in B.C. Memoir 5, 1964 (Victoria: Provincial Museum of Natural History and Anthropology, 1964), p. 41.

[23] Thomas Crosby, *Among the An-ko-me-nums* (Toronto: William Briggs, 1907), p. 68.

[24] Margaret Ormsby, *British Columbia: A History* (Vancouver: Macmillan Company of Canada, 1958), pp. 127-128.

[25] Hills, Journals, p. 214, Synod Archives; and Fluke, "Early Days," *British Columbia Historical Quarterly* pp. 183-185.

[26] *Colonist,* April 10, 1863, p. 3.

[27] *Colonist,* April 9 and 28, May 4 and 19, 1863, all p. 3.

[28] James Douglas to the Duke of Newcastle, May 21, 1863, CO 305/20, pp. 177-185, Public Records Office, mf.

[29] *Colonist,* May 6, June 26, July 6, 1863, all p. 3; and Douglas to Newcastle, May 21, May 30 and July 4, 1863, CO 305/20, pp. 177-185, 191-193 and 223-234, PRO. mf.

[30] *Colonist,* April 10, 1863, p. 3.

[31] *Colonist,* July 26, 1863, p. 3.

[32] *Colonist,* July 9, 1870, p. 3.

[33] Philip I. Hankin to A. Nicholson, J. O'Brien, and others, July 11, 1870, CO 2/505, Colonial Correspondence (hereafter cited as CC), PABC: and R. McMillan to Augustus F. Pemberton, Police Commissioner, Victoria July 18, 1870, Superintendent of Police correspondence outgoing, GR 61, PABC.

[34] James McNamara and W. Edwards to A. T. Bushby, November 18, 1870, F511(2), CC, PABC.

[35] Matthew Baillie Begbie to Colonial Secretary P. Hankin, November, 1870, court notes and correspondence, Matthew Baillie Begbie Correspondence, 142(i), CC, PABC. Robert Bishop to P. Hankin, December 1870, 153, CC, PABC; and *Colonist,* April 30, 1873, p. 3. See also Pemberton to Hankin, November 24, December 7, 16 and 22, 1870, GR 61, PABC.

[36] *Colonist,* September 16, 1871, p. 3.

[37] *Colonist,* April 30, May 1, 4 and 6, 1873, all p. 3. Charges were to have been laid against Sophie's assailant (who had been apprehended by special constable Henry Clapham) as soon as she recovered, but no record can be found of this case being heard in Victoria court.

[38] Interview with Wilbert Deacon, Mayne Island, November, 1981. Wilbert Deacon is the grandson of pioneer resident John and Margaret Deacon, Village Bay.

[39] Robin Fisher, *Contact and Conflict* (Vancouver: University of British Columbia Press, 1977), p. 113.

[40] Hills, Journals, p. 215, Synod Archives.

[41] Christian Mayer's common-law wife Mathilda verified from probated will 4755, Court Registry, Victoria. Mathilda lived with Mayers for at least ten years while their three sons, George, Joseph and Frederick were born. Robert Clarke's wife Annie verified by corresponding, Begbie to P. Hankin, November 1870, CC, 142 (I), PABC; John Silva's wife Louisa verified by Leo and Gayla Nelson, "Silva Family," typescript, Add. MS 242, PABC; Henry Georgeson's wife Sophie verified by great granddaughter Mary Ellen Harding, Galiano; William Collinson's wife Mary verified by great granddaughter Margaret Bennett, Mayne Island; and Jacob Heck's wife Kitty verified by Vera Greene, granddaughter of William and Ann Robson, Mayne Island.

[42] Interview with Edith Higginbottom, August 1981, Mayne Island. Edith is the granddaughter of Thomas and Alice Bennett.

[43] *Colonist,* March 28, 1863, p. 2.

[44] Barry M. Gough, *The Royal Navy and the Northwest Coast of North America, 1810-1914* (Vancouver: University of British Columbia Press, 1974), pp. 89-92. See also R. Byron Johnson, *Very Far West Indeed* (London: Sampson Low, Marson Low & Searle, 1872), pp. 158-159. Johnson describes being pursued by Indians across Georgia Strait to Plumper Pass in 1862, where naval gunboats were anchored. F. W. Howay and Hubert Howe Bancroft suggest that Johnson had a powerful imagination and did not even come to British Columbia until 1863. (See: *British Columbia from the Earliest Times to the Present* 2 (Vancouver: S. J. Clarke Publishing Co., 1914), 675, and *The Works of Hubert Howe Bancroft* (San Francisco: The History Company, 1887), p. 771.

[45] T. R. Figg, "Mayne Island, Interesting Letter from that Flourishing Locality," *Colonist,* September 8, 1885, p. 3.

46 Indians of the Chilcotin country remained hostile towards white settlers for more than a decade, beginning with the massacre of thirteen white men, part of a road party working on the Homathko River, in April 1864. (Fisher, *Contact and Conflict,* pp. 107-108 and 184-185.)

47 British Columbia, Legal Surveys Branch, Ministry of Lands, Parks and Housing, pre-emption records for the Cowichan land district; and Registration of Pre-emption Claims, Department of Lands and Works, Inventory II, 1861-1870, GR 765, PABC.

48 Ibid., and F. W. Laing, "Colonial Settlers," unpublished manuscript, Add. MS 700 (A-819), pp. 11 and 43, PABC, See also "Boone Helme," *Victoria Times,* August 18, 1893, p. 7; and *Cariboo Sentinel,* May 6, 1867, p. 3, and May 15, 1868, p. 3.

Greavy and Mayers may not have intended to settle permanently on Mayne Island, for both men were employed in the late 1860's as engineers on Fraser River steamboats, Greavy at Soda Creek where he died *(Colonist,* September 6, 1867), and Mayers at New Westminster (*Sessional Papers,* 1879, Voter's List — New Westminster District, p. 115). Greavy also owned a lot in Victoria. Prominent Victoria lawyer and politician Montague Tyrwhitt Drake purchased both the lot and pre-emption rights to the Mayne Island property from the estate in February 1871, following Greavy's death (intestate papers of James Messenger Greavy, Court Registry, Victoria).

49 Laing, "Colonial Settlers," p. 332, PABC.

50 Ibid., p. 194; C. Brew to Colonial Secretary, June 6, 1865, enclosing Collinson's sketch of proposed pre-emption at Sumas, CC F194(I), PABC; and Cowichan land register, Legal Surveys Branch, Ministry of Lands, Parks and Housing, Victoria.

51 Leo and Gayla Nelson, "Silva Family," typescript, Add. MS 242, PABC.

52 *British Columbia Gazette,* November 27, 1875, p. 263; January 1, 1876, p. 4; and February 28, 1880, p. 121.

53 British Columbia Land Ordinance, 1870, cited by Robert E. Cail, *Land Man and the Law* (Vancouver: University of British Columbia Press, 1974), pp. 252-253.

54 William T. Collinson to Governor Frederick Seymour, March 24, 1867, CC F315(I), PABC.

CHAPTER II

1 Wharf noted in Report of Public Works, British Columbia *Sessional Paper,* 1878, p. 820.

2 Jonathan Begg was providing a postal service for northern Salt Spring Island in 1859 (Fluke, "Early Days," p. 180), but an official post office was not recognized by the federal government until 1874. (George H. Melvin, *The Post Offices of British Columbia* [Vernon: Wayside Press, 1972], p. 2.) Petition of Mayne Island residents to the Honorable Postmaster General, October 1876, and covering report 251, R. Wallace, post office inspector, Victoria, to Postmaster General, RG3, 6, Public Archives Canada (hereafter cited as PAC). Wallace to Postmaster General, June 4, 1880, inspector's report 534, RG 3, 6, PAC. Information on Collinson's house from Margaret Bennett, Mayne Island, January 1982. Collinson moved from his first pre-emption on Mayne Island to Miners Bay about 1880.

3 Post office inspector, Victoria, to Postmaster General, Ottawa, reports 885 and 936, RG 3, 6, PAC. Collinson requested $200 a year salary when the 2 a.m. sailing was inaugurated. He was granted $150.

4 *Saanich Peninsula and Gulf Islands Review,* December 2, 1953, pp. 1 and 7 (hereafter cited as *Sidney Review); and Colonist,* May 26, 1892, p. 1.

5 Public Schools Report, *Sessional Papers,* 1883, pp. 106 and 117; 1885, p. 92; "Mayne Island School Examination," *Colonist,* July 1, 1884, p. 3; and *Colonist,* June 28, 1885, p. 3. The Galiano School was opened in November 1892, and the Pender Island School in August 1894.

6 "Mayne Island Festivities Incidental to the Opening of the New Wharf," *Colonist,* December 11, 1885, p. 3.

7 Ibid.

8 George Hearn and David Wilkie, *The Cordwood Limited* (Victoria: Fleming Review Printing Ltd., 1974), pp. 16-55; and F. W. Howay, *British Columbia,* 2:435.

9 British Columbia *Sessional Papers,* 1893, p. 871. Canada, *Census,* 1891.

10 Bancroft relates the story of apple seeds being planted at Fort Vancouver, having been brought to the Fort in the pocket of Captain Simpson, from England. *Bancroft's Works* 28 (San Francisco: A. L. Bancroft and Company, 1884), 441. Derek Reimer, ed., "Farming — 'In a Mild Sort of Fashion'," *The Gulf Islanders,* Vol. 5, no. 4, Sound Heritage (Victoria Provincial Archives of British Columbia, 1976), p. 43; Maragret A. Ormsby, "The History of Agriculture in B. C.," *Scientific Agriculture,* 20, p. 65; *Colonist,* February 19, 1896, p. 3.

11 British Columbia, *Sessional Papers,* 1878-1900, passim.

[12] Charles Groth, Diary, passim., PABC.

[13] Ibid, and pp. 1, 28 and 51.

[14] Henry Georgeson, Diary, in the possession of great granddaughter, Mary Ellen Harding, Galiano Island.

[15] Cicely Lyons, *Salmon: Our Heritage* (Vancouver: Mitchell Press, 1969), pp. 165-189; and David J. Reid, *The Development of the Fraser River Salmon Canning Industry, 1885-1913* (n.p.: Department of the Environment, 1873), p. 72. Charles Groth, Diary pp. 6, 31, 47 and 119, PABC.

[16] Charles Groth, Diary, pp. 70 and 91-93, PABC; and British Columbia *Sessional Papers,* 1885, p. 255.

[17] Charles Groth, Diary, p. 105, PABC.

[18] *Colonist,* March 12, 1867, p. 3; and F. S. Hussey, Superintendent of Provincial Police, to William Robson, Mayne Island, November 28, 1893. Provincial Police, correspondence outgoing, GR 61, PABC.

[19] William McNeill to Hussey, September 14, October 15 and 24, 1893, Provincial Police, incoming correspondence, GR 55, PABC.

[20] Arthur Drummond to Hussey, August 7, 1894, GR 55, PABC.

[21] G. E. Mortimore, "He Never Fired His Gun," *Colonist,* September 15, 1957, p. 14; Drummond to Hussey, October 8, 1894, GR 55, PABC.

[22] Angus Ego to Hussey, June 22, 1903, GR 55, PABC; Hussey to Stephen Hoskins, September 15, 1898, GR 61, PABC.

[23] Drummond to Hussey, January 16, 1897; and Hoskins to Hussey, December 21, 1899, GR 55, PABC.

[24] *Vancouver Daily Province,* October 23, 1903, p. 1, November 4, 1903, p. 7.

[25] Mortimore, *Colonist,* September 15, 1957, p. 14.

[26] Drummond to Hussey, May 22, 1896, GR 55, PABC.

[27] Winifred Grey, Diary, pp. 461-462, Add MSS 604/A-791, PABC; David Richardson, *Pig War Islands* (East Sound, Wash.: Orcas Publishing Company, 1971), pp. 271-273.

[28] Winifred Grey, Diary, p. 487, PABC.

[29] Thomas M. Robb to Hussey, July 1, 1893, GR 55, PABC.

[30] Winifred Grey, Diary, p. 451, PABC; Mortimore, *Colonist,* September 15, 1957, p. 14.

[31] Hussey to William Robson, Mayne Island, November 28, 1893, GR 61, PABC; Drummond to Hussey, September 8 and 16, 1896, GR 55, PABC; and British Columbia *Sessional Papers,* 1896, p. 309.

[32] Drummond to Hussey, February 8, 1897, GR 55, PABC. *Colonist,* February 3 and February 10, 1897, p. 3.

[33] Hussey to Drummond, February 8, 1897, GR 61, PABC; and Ego to Hussey, March 3, 1901, GR 55, PABC.

[34] Henry Georgeson, Diary, entry for December 26, 1912.

[35] British Columbia, *Sessional Papers,* 1885, p. 255.

[36] John O'Hara to Colin S. Campbell, Acting Superintendent of Police, September 30, 1911, GR 55, PABC.

[37] Without extensive research it is difficult to verify when the Provincial Police finally provided a patrol launch for the Salt Spring constable, but most likely this important asset was granted in the 1920's, during the rum running era.

[38] Canon William Francis Locke Paddon, parochial notes; and Church Register, St. Mary Magdalene Church, Mayne Island. Also, Charles Groth Diary, p. 68, PABC.

[39] T. R. Figg, *Colonist,* September 2, 1885, p. 3; and Paddon, parochial notes.

[40] *Colonist,* August 30, 1893, p. 2, and August 3, 1901, p. 4.

[41] Beatrice J. S. Freeman, ed., *A Gulf Islands Patchwork* (Victoria: Fleming Review Printing, 1974), p. 47; Winifred Grey, Diary, p. 650, PABC.

[42] Robson's hotel contained a large ballroom that was referred to as Robson's hall in newspaper accounts of early dances on Mayne Island, but the first reference to the Mayne Island community hall is in Winifred Grey's diary. Winifred noted that Mrs. Robson and Mrs. Bennett had given the Greys a wedding reception there in July, 1900. Grey, diary, p. 580, PABC; "Declaration of Association," Maple Leaf Club, 1903, in possession of Mayne Island Agricultural Association, Mayne Island.

[43] Winifred Grey, Diary, p. 653, PABC.

[44] Interviews with Fred Bennett and Wilbert Deacon, Mayne Island, and *Colonist,* June 9, 1894, p. 3, describes the deaths of Joseph Bodine and Harry Georgeson off coast of Japan.

[45] Interview with Margaret Bennett, Mayne Island.

[46] Church Register, St. Mary Magdalene Church; and *Sidney Review,* August 24, 1960, p. 13.

[47] Elizabeth's death was published in Vancouver *Daily World,* July 29, 1899, p. 8. Charles Groth's diary records the birth of the first baby at New Westminster, and the births of the next three children at home. Charles Groth, Diary, frontspiece, PABC.

[48] Freeman, ed., *Patchwork,* p. 184; interview with Geraldine Goldsmith, March 1982, Victoria, granddaughter of Emma Higgs, South Pender Island.

[49] *Sidney Review,* April 16, 1958, p. 1; Freeman, ed., Patchwork, p. 130, and Winifred Grey, Diary, p. 563, PABC.

[50] Henry Georgeson, Diary, entry for November 28, 1913; interview with Vera Greene, Mayne Island, January 1982.

[51] Freeman, ed., *Patchwork,* p. 171.

[52] *Colonist,* February 28, 1895, p. 3, and March 6, 1895, p. 7. In 1955 Margaret Bennett, when proprietor of Springwater Lodge, Mayne Island, had as a guest a man who claimed he was the grandson of Nicholson. The visitor spent several days "prospecting" the site of Nicholson's homestead.

[53] Freeman, ed., *Patchwork,* pp. 11 and 85; and Winifred Grey, diary, p. 549, PABC. Also interview with Mrs. Muriel Page, Victoria, September 1981. The Chicago World's Fair, in 1893 was an international event that also caught the imagination of Gulf Island residents. Some furs were sent to the exhibition from Mayne Island, and two residents, James Bennett and William Deacon, attended the exhibition. *Colonist,* April 25, 1893, p. 2.

[54] Winifred Grey, Diary, p. 485, PABC.

[55] T. R. Figg, *Colonist,* September 2, 1885, p. 3.

[56] Thomas Bennett to Premier William Smithe, June 20, 1883, Smithe Papers, correspondence inward, EC/SM 62, PABC.

[57] Post office inspector's reports, Victoria to Postmaster General, Ottawa, 1887, 794 and 814, RG 3, 6, PAC.

[58] Correspondence, Rudd, vs. Collinson, British Columbia, *Sessional Papers,* 1897, pp. 933-943.

[59] Tom retained his zest for life as long as he lived. Shortly before his death in 1911 he wrote to his daughter Emma, that he was planning to move to the South Seas as soon as his health permitted. Letter in the possession of Margaret Bennett, Mayne Island.

[60] *Colonist,* August 17, 1883, p. 3; and Robert Connell "Among the Gulf Islands," *Colonist,* September 25, 1938, p. 3.

[61] Puetz's store is mentioned in Groth Diary, passim., PABC, and also in reports from Post Office inspector, Victoria to Ottawa 1887, 794 and 814 RG3, 6, PAC. Enlarged Mayne Island Hotel verified by photographs in possession of Margaret Bennett and Vera Greene, Mayne Island. Point Comfort Hotel described in *Colonist,* October 18, 1892, p. 7.

[62] *Colonist,* October 18, 1892, p. 7, and June 30, 1897, p. 5. See also Reimer, ed., "In the Grand Style: The Point Comfort Hotel," pp. 49-53. Reimer gives 1900 as the date that Maude purchased Point Comfort Hotel, but liquor licences, recorded in the Superintendent of Police correspondence, GR 55, suggest 1902. Petitions against liquor licence for Robson's Hotel also in GR 55. Prohibition vote in *Sidney Review,* September 21, 1916, p. 1.

[63] Photograph by Hannah Maynard, Victoria, ca. 1895.

[64] New Westminster *Columbian,* July 7, 1897.

[65] Buckham Collection, 65:14, Add. MS 436, PABC. There was also a minor flurry of coal speculation in 1893, which resulted in the entire land area of Mayne being bonded. *Colonist,* July 6, 1893, p. 2.

[66] Reminiscences of Harold Payne, formerly of Saturna, *Sidney Review,* April 5, 1950, pp. 1 and 6. Photograph of schooner loaded with cordwood in Richard Mouat Toynbee, *Snapshots of Early Salt Spring and Other Favoured Islands* (Victoria: Morriss Printing Company, Ltd., 1978), p. 69. Report of mine explosion on Tumbo in *Victoria Daily Times,* February 1, 1893, p. 7. Statistics regarding woodcutters cited in Report of Immigration Office, British Columbia *Sessional Papers,* 1902, p. 851.

[67] Harold Payne, *Sidney Review,* April 5, 1950, pp. 1 and 6. A Mr. Mikuni, presumably Japanese, also shipped cordwood and charcoal from his pre-emption on Saturna, and James Bennett of Mayne obtained a contract from a Fraser River cannery. *Colonist,* passim, 1893-1895.

[68] British Columbia, *Sessional Papers,* 1902, p. 851.

[69] John Nagata to Author, December 1981.

[70] Freeman, ed., *Patchwork,* pp. 176-177; and Reimer "Englishness," pp. 11-15.

[71] See: W. Peter Ward, *White Canada Forever* (Montreal: McGill-Queen's University Press, 1978), pp. 129-131, and 53-76. Also Ken Adachi, *The Enemy That Never Was* (Toronto: McClelland and Stewart, 1976); Ann Gomer Sunahara, *The Politics of Racism* (Toronto: James Lorimer & Company, 1981); and Patricia E. Roy, "British Columbia's Fear of Asians 1900-1950," *Social History* 13 (May 1980):

161-172. The first subdivisions are noted in the *Colonist*, March 1, 1893, p. 2.

[72] The Mayne Island population for 1900 is based on the residents listed in Williams' *British Columbia Directory*, 1899 (Vancouver: Province Publishing Co. Ltd., 1899), p. 217.

CHAPTER III

[1] Robert Turner, *The Pacific Princesses* (Victoria: Sono Nis Press, 1977), pp. 233-239, and passim.

[2] Norman R. Hacking and W. Kaye Lamb, *The Princess Story* (Vancouver: Mitchell Press Limited, 1974), pp. 236-346, and passim.

[3] Hearn and Wilkie, *The Cordwood Limited*, pp. 16-55.

[4] Freeman, ed., *Patchwork*, pp. 23, 81 and 183.

[5] Interview with Muriel Page, Victoria, May 1981. Mrs. Page lived on Galiano from 1898 to 1900, and on Mayne from 1900 to 1904.

[6] Freeman, ed., *Patchwork*, p. 23.

[7] Mayne, *Four Years*, p. 207.

[8] *Colonist*, February 20, 1872, p. 3; and diorama, Mayne Island Museum. The wreckage site off Georgina Shoals has now been designated a provincial heritage site, thereby protecting it from vandalism by divers. *(Victoria Daily Times,* February 4, 1977, p. 2, and February 7, p. 1.)

[9] Transport Canada, Victoria, File 8010-1972; and *Sidney Review*, October 3, 1922, p. 1. Henry Georgeson was presented with the Imperial Long Service Medal for 37 years in the lighthouse service in October, 1922.

[10] *Victoria Daily Times*, January 12, 1916, p. 8.

[11] *Colonist*, April 2 and April 14, 1916, both p. 11; and *Victoria Daily Times*, July 17, 1916, p. 8.

[12] Leo and Gayla Nelson, "Silva Family," PABC: *Sidney Review*, January 2, 1935, and August 18, 1937, both p. 1.

[13] *Colonist*, February 2, 1902, p. 9; *Province*, April 5, 1906, p. 1, and November 27, 1907, p. 1.

[14] Freeman, ed., *Patchwork*, p. 27; *Sidney Review*, April 28 and September 1, 1921, both p. 5; *Farm and Home*, November 16, 1922, p. 6. For information regarding the earlier growing season on the Gulf Islands see B. J. Yorke and G. A. Kendall, *Daily Bright Sunshine, 1941-1970* (Ontario: Atmospheric and Environment Services, Canada, 1972).

[15] *Sidney Review*, September 29, 1957, pp. 1 and 4; and Freeman, *Patchwork*, pp. 12, 21 and 118. The importance of the Salt Spring Island Creamery to the smaller Gulf Island farms was confirmed by an interview with Reginald Cousens, Courtenay, whose farm on Mayne Island shipped cream to Salt Spring between 1914 and 1920.

[16] *Colonist*, April 21, 1923, p. 5. Director W. Sutherland hoped that the output could double in 1923 and he was seeking more outlets on Vancouver Island.

[17] Freeman, ed., *Patchwork*, pp. 51-52; A. F. Fluke, "Early Days," p. 180; and Bea Hamilton, *Salt Spring Island*, p. 35. Information on the brick plant was obtained from interviews with Edith Higginbottom and Fred Bennett, Mayne Island. The provincial government Companies Office has a record of the Franco-Canadian Company, but the brick yard enterprise is not detailed.

[18] Reimer, ed., "In the Grand Style," pp. 49-50. Bricks were made and shipped for only a brief period.

[19] Jesse Brown, ed., *Mayne Island Fall Fair Centennial Booklet*, p. 25; and *Sidney Review*, May 17, 1923, p.3, and September 17, 1923, p. 5.

[20] Interview with Margaret Bennett, Mayne Island, November 1981; Grandview Lodge register for 1925 and brochure for Lodge, ca. 1934, in the possession of Margaret Bennett.

[21] Weekly reports on Mayne Island for the period 1920-1940, *Sidney Review*. Nellie McClung's description of her visit to Grandview Lodge was found in an undated newspaper clipping in Emma Naylor's papers, now in the possession of Margaret Bennett.

[22] *Sidney Review*, April 28, 1943, p. 5.

[23] Pamela Roberts to author, February 28, 1981; and Nancy Rainsford, "The Anchorage, 1936-1952," *Mayne Island Community News*, September 1979, p. 1.

[24] Weekly reports on Mayne Island for the period 1940-1950, *Sidney Review*.

[25] Reimer, ed., "In the Grand Style," pp. 49-50; *Sidney Review*, June 24, 1953, p. 5; Lukin Johnston, *Beyond the Rockies* (Toronto: J. M. Dent and Sons Limited, 1929), pp. 8-9.

[26] Ibid.; Interview with Muriel Page, May 1981; and Winifred Grey, Diary, p. 487, PABC.

[27] Weekly reports on Mayne Island for the period 1920-1935, *Sidney Review*. Mrs. Maude was the island correspondent for the *Sidney Review* during this period.

[28] Paddon, parochial notes.

[29] Interview with Nancy Rainsford, Mayne Island, February 1982. Nancy is the daughter of Richard Hall. *Sidney Review,* April 28, 1921, p. 5.

[30] Weekly reports on Mayne Island for the period 1920-1940, *Sidney Review.*

[31] Ibid.

[32] Ibid.; *Colonist,* October 19, 1898, p. 6, September 28, 1892, p. 2, October 11, 1893, p. 2; annual Fall Fair brochures, Mayne Island, issued for most years between 1925 and 1982, Mayne Island Museum.

[33] Freeman, ed., *Patchwork,* p. 164; interviews with Fred Bennett and Edith Higginbottom, February 1982.

[34] Interviews with Fred Bennett and Edith Higginbottom, February 1982, and weekly reports on Mayne Island, 1920-1940, *Sidney Review.*

By 1916 only twelve Indians were living on the Helen Point Reserve (with four heads of families). Their chief occupation was fishing and their living conditions were described as "fairly prosperous and comfortable." The children attended the Kuper Island Industrial School, not the Mayne Island public school. The only other permanently occupied Indian Reserve in the Gulf Islands was at Fulford Harbour, Salt Spring Island. Reserves on Valdes Island at Porlier Pass, and on Pender Island were occupied occasionally, and the Reserve at East Point, Saturna, was vacant. [*Report of the Royal Commission on Indian Affairs for the Province of British Columbia* (Victoria: King's Printer, 1916), pp. 277, 280, 281, 285, 287, 293, 294 and 301.]

[35] Register, St. Mary Magdalene Church, Mayne Island.

[36] See, for example, Margaret Ormsby, *British Columbia: A History,* pp. 107, 257, 494; and Jean Barman, "The World that British Settlers Made: Class, Ethnicity and Private Education in the Okanagan Valley," in W. Peter Ward and Robert A. J. Mcdonald, ed., *British Columbia: Historical Readings* (Vancouver: Douglas and McIntyre Ltd., 1981), pp. 600-626.

[37] Freeman, ed., *Patchwork,* p. 189; and undated newspaper clipping found in Emma Naylor's papers.

[38] Interview with Fred Bennett, November 1981, regarding Frank Heck's car; the *Sidney Review,* January 10, 1922, p. 5, describes the seven cars on Mayne; the first airplane is cited in parish notes for St. Mary Magdalene Church; and Dalton Hill's new crystal set is mentioned in *Sidney Review,* June 26, 1924, p. 5. The telephone service in 1911 is noted in John O'Hara to Superintendent of Provincial Police, Hussey, September 30, 1911, GR 55, PABC. The erection of the transmitting station is described in *Sidney Review,* November 28, 1929, p. 5.

[39] *Sidney Review,* September 28, 1922, August 7, 1924 and May 22, 1935, all p. 5.

[40] *Colonist,* October 14, 1919, p. 2, and December 3, 1922, p. 27; *Sidney Review,* April 14, 1921 and April 13, 1923, both p. 5, describe the Board of Trade. See *Vancouver Province,* September 20, 1925, p. 2; and Lukin Johnston, "Letters from the Gulf Islands," *Vancouver Province,* June 5, 1927, p.3, for journalist reports.

[41] El Madrona Sanitarium Ltd., Vancouver, undated prospectus, Mayne Island Museum. For information about the proposed CPR hotel, see *Sidney Review,* May 13, 1959, p. 5.

[42] Geoff Story, "The Steeles — A Success Story," and Harold Neale, "A Brief History of the Cannery on Mayne Island," in Jesse Brown, ed., Mayne Island Fall Fair Centennial Booklet, pp. 4-5.

[43] *Sidney Review,* passim. See especially the Victoria Day account of May 28, 1921, p. 5. Maude's adventure, which ended off the coast of California, is detailed in James H. Hamilton, *Western Shores* (Vancouver: Progress Publishing Co. Ltd., 1932), pp. 67-70. Maude was hit on the head by the boom of the *Half Moon,* his 22 ft. boat, and forced to return home.

[44] Ibid., and interview with Fred Bennett, Mayne Island, November 1981.

[45] *Sidney Review,* May 19, 1937, p. 3.

[46] Ibid., June 7, 1939, p. 1.

[47] *Colonist,* December 27, 1936, p. 3 (ms); interview, Fred and Margaret Bennett, November 1981.

[48] John Nagata, "The Japanese People," and Margaret Bennett, "Japanese Story," in Brown, ed., *Mayne Island Fall Fair Centennial Booklet,* pp. 22-23; also F. W. Pratt, "Japanese at Horton Bay, Mayne Island," in Spalding, ed., *Patchwork,* pp. 176-177.

[49] *Vancouver Province,* May 12, 1934, p. 6 (ms).

[50] This estimate is based upon interviews with William Deacon, and with Fred and Margaret Bennett who operated four of the greenhouses after the Japanese were relocated in 1942. The estimate is confirmed by John Nagata, Mayne Island, who owned a hothouse on Mayne Island, and whose father, Kumazo Nagata, was the secretary of the hothouse co-operative, the Active Pass Growers Association. (Letter to the author, December 1981.) Population estimate obtained from RCMP report to Hugh Keenlyside, Chairman, Board of Review, September 20, 1938. (Department of Immigration file C 4752, microfilm, PABC.) The report stated that of 186 people on Mayne Island, 62 were Japanese.

[51] Canada, Parliament, House of Commons, *Debates* (Ottawa: King's Printer, May 18, 1939, p. 4036); Adachi, *The Enemy That Never Was,* pp. 204-205.

[52] *Colonist,* March 31, 1931, p. 2.

[53] "M.L.A. Urges Immediate Census of all Nipponese," *Vancouver Sun,* January 19, 1938, p. 1.

[54] Ibid., and *Vancouver Province,* January 19, 1938, pp. 1-2.

[55] Interview with Fred Bennett, November 1981, and voting results published in *Sidney Review,* June 9, 1937, p. 1.

[56] Charles Flick, "Japanese on Mayne Island," *Colonist,* January 25, 1938, p. 4.

[57] Inspector G. W. Fish, RCMP, to Board of Review, September 20, 1938, Department of Immigration file C 4752, microfilm, PABC. By 1938 the Japanese had grouped together on either Salt Spring or Mayne Island. There was one couple living by themselves on North Pender, and the other exceptions were the seasonally operated herring salteries on North Pender and Galiano Islands. (John Nagata to author, December 1981.)

[58] Nagata to author, December 1981, and interview with Fred Bennett, November 1981. The building and heating system were purchased from Richard Hall for Nagata's greenhouses. Interview with Nancy Rainsford, April 1983.

[59] Forest E. LaViolette, *The Canadian Japanese and World War II* (Toronto: University of Toronto Press, 1948), pp. 46-47.

[60] Interview with Fred Bennett, November 1981, and Toyo Takata, *Nikkei Legacy* (Toronto: New Canada Publications, 1983), p. 110.

[61] LaViolette, *The Canadian Japanese,* pp. 54-55, and Sunahara, *The Politics of Racism,* pp. 31-45.

[62] *Sidney Review,* March 25, 1942, p. 2.

[63] Kumazo Nagata to British Columbia Security Commission, April 15, 1942, RG 36/27, 9, file 208, PAC. This file is restricted and Mr. John Nagata has given permission for the re-production of his father's letter. Nagata to author, December 1981.

[64] *Colonist,* January 4, 1942, p. 20.

[65] Ibid.

[66] *Vancouver Province,* April 20, 1942, p. 2; and interview with Don and Gertrude Vigurs, Mayne Island, February 1975, and with Fred and Margaret Bennett, November 1981. The Vigurs and Bennetts witnessed the Japanese departure on the *Princess Mary,* April 21.

[67] Nagata to author, November 1981; interview with Fred Bennett, November 1981; and Mayne Island School records, School District No. 64, Ganges, B. C.

[68] Nagata to author, November 1981.

[69] *Report of the Department of Labour on the Administration of Japanese Affairs in Canada 1942-1944* (np: King's Printer, 1944), pp. 26-27.

[70] Kamiaki Nakashima, "Economic Aspects of Japanese Evacuation from the Canadian Pacific Coast," (Thesis, McGill University, 1946), p. 123.

[71] *Sidney Review,* November 24, 1943, p. 2, and December 8, 1943, p. 5; interview with Fred Bennett, November 1981.

[72] Interview with Fred Bennett, November 1981.

[73] Nakashima, "Economic Aspects," p. 123.

[74] Canada, Parliament, House of Commons, *Debates* (Ottawa: King's Printer, April 9, 1946), p. 703.

[75] Personal knowledge.

[76] For example, Kumazo Nagata was awarded slightly more than one third of his claim, and Kumajiro Konishi less than one sixth of his claim. (Recommendations for Payment of Awards by Justice H. I. Bird, Japanese Canadian Citizens Association, MC 28, v. 7, PAC.)
Torzo Iwasaki v. The Queen (1969) I Exchequer Court Reports 281; and Supreme Court of Canada, 1970, Supreme Court Reports 437-438.

[77] Interview with Fred Bennett, November 1981.

[78] *Sidney Review,* December 10, 1941, p. 1.

[79] Interview with J. Hawthorne, Galiano, and Gordon Robson, Mayne Island, December 1981. Both men took part in the militia for the outer Gulf Islands.

[80] *Sidney Review,* October 30, 1940, p. 5, and passim. 1940-1945; interview with Margaret Bennett, November 1981.

[81] Interviews with Fred Bennett and Wilbert Deacon, November 1981.

[82] Freeman, ed., *Patchwork,* pp. 187-189; and *Sidney Review,* June 2, 1943, p. 5, June 1, 1951, p. 5, and September 30, 1953, p. 1.

[83] Register, St. Mary Magdalene Church; and interview with Margaret Bennett, November 1981.

[84] Mayne Island Parent-Teachers' Association records for period 1945-1955, provided by Elsie Wilks, Mayne Island.

[85] *Sidney Review,* August 4, 1948, p. 1.

[86] Weekly reports on Mayne Island for the period 1920-1950, *Sidney Review.*

[87] *Sidney Review,* September 9, 1949, p. 1; September 14, 1949, p. 1; and January 18 and 25, 1950, both p. 1.

[88] *Sidney Review,* March 14, 1951, p. 1.

CHAPTER IV

[1] *Sidney Review,* December 5, 1951, p. 1.

[2] Turner, *The Pacific Princesses,* pp. 235 and 237; and *Sidney Review,* April 22, 1953, p. 1.

[3] Captain J. Hamilton, Marine Supertintendent, Canadian Pacific Railway, to Captain I. G. Denroche, Secretary, Gulf Islands Improvement Bureau, December 5, 1951, CPR Archives, Montreal.

[4] Ivan G. Denroche to Hon. Alphonse Fournier, Minister of Public Works, December 27, 1951, CPR Archives, Montreal.

[5] *Sidney Review,* March 26, 1952 and July 12, 1952, both p. 1.

[6] Vancouver *News Herald,* October 1952, and *Sidney Review,* January 21, 1953, p. 1.

[7] Turner, *Pacific Princesses,* p. 202.

[8] *Vancouver Province,* September 4, 1953, p. 11.

[9] *Colonist,* September 4, 1953, p. 4.

[10] Harold Neale, "Brief History of the Cannery," in Brown, ed., *Mayne Island Fall Fair Centennial Booklet, p. 5.*

[11] *Sidney Review,* September 23, 1953, p. 1.

[12] Vancouver *News Herald,* September 9, 1953.

[13] *Sidney Review,* October 28, 1953, p. 1.

[14] Turner, *Pacific Princesses,* p. 204.

[15] *Sidney Review,* September 23, 1953, p. 1.

[16] *Colonist,* October 30, 1953, p. 15; and *Sidney Review,* February 17, 1954, p. 1.

[17] *Sidney Review,* February 24, 1954, p. 1; and interview with William Wilks, May 1982. Bill Wilks was a member of many delegations that consulted with the provincial government regarding ferry services to the Gulf Islands between 1950 and 1961. He remembers this period as being very frustrating for Gulf Islands residents.

[18] *Sidney Review,* September 22, 1954, p. 1, and November 24, 1954, p. 1; and Philip A. Gaglardi, Minister of Highways, to Mrs. Virginia Shirley, Port Washington, September 15, 1954, advising that negotiations between Black Ball Ferries and the Gulf Island Ferry Company had reached a stalemate, Dept. of Highways, File 4227, section 1, Victoria. Neill's poem also in File 4227.

[19] *Sidney Review,* March 16, 1955, p. 1.

[20] George Pearson to P. A. Gaglardi, May 25, 1955, Dept. of Highways, File 4227, section 1.

[21] *Sidney Review,* May 17, 1955, p. 1, June 1, 1955, p. 1; and Dr. J. B. Hallowes, Saturna, to P. A. Gaglardi, May 25, 1955, Dept. of Highways, File 4227, section 1.

[22] Miss A. E. Scoones, Executive Secretary, Gulf Islands Improvement Bureau, to P. A. Gaglardi, September 14, 1955; O. New to P. A. Gaglardi, September 21 and 26, 1955; and petition from North and South Pender Islands to P. A. Gaglardi, October 17, 1955. Department of Highways File 4227, section 2.

[23] *Sidney Review,* February 15, 1956, p. 1.

[24] New was not interested in submitting a bid for a subsidized service, hence Mouat's bid was accepted. Interview with Sparkie New, June 1982.

[25] *Sidney Review,* February 1, 1956, p. 1; and Department of Highways File 4227, section 2.

[26] *Sidney Review,* July 4, 1956, p. 1.

[27] W. A. C. Bennett to P. A. Gaglardi, July 9, 1956.

[28] *Sidney Review,* September 26, 1956, p. 1.

[29] *Sidney Review,* December 19, 1956, pp. 1 and 7; Earle C. Westwood to P. A. Gaglardi, January 3, 1957; George Paulin to P. A. Gaglardi, January 21, 1957; and Order-in-Council dated February 11, 1957, approving $500 monthly subsidy for 12 months to Coast Ferries, effective February 1, 1957, Department of Highways File 4227, section 3.

[30] *Sidney Review,* February 13, 1957, p. 1.

[31] *Sidney Review,* August 7, 1957, p. 1, as reported by the Dominion Bureau of Statistics.

[32] Pender Islands Farmers Institute to P. A. Gaglardi, October 3, 1957, and November 14, 1957, Department of Highways File 4227, section 4; *Sidney Review,* September 29, 1957.

[33] *Sidney Review,* November 13, 1957, p. 1.

[34] *Sidney Review,* June 19, 1957, p. 1, and October 23, 1957, p. 1.

[35] *Sidney Review,* September 24, 1958, p. 1.

[36] *Sidney Review,* December 16, 1959, p. 1.

[37] Brief to the Executive Council, February 26, 1960, from Gulf Island Navigation Ltd., Legislative Library, Parliament Buildings, Victoria, B. C.

[38] *Sidney Review,* July 13, 1960, p. 1, and July 20, 1960, pp. 9 and 10.

[39] Ferry schedule in *Sidney Review,* July and August, 1960.

[40] *Sidney Review,* October 13, 1960, p. 8.

[41] *Sidney Review,* October 26, 1960; December 14, 1960, February 1, 1961 and February 22, 1961, all page 1.

[42] *Sidney Review,* March 1, 1961, p. 1.

[43] Interview with W. Wilks, Mayne Island, November 1981; and with O. New, January 1982; and *Sidney Review,* July 26, 1961, pp. 1 and 7.

[44] *Sidney Review,* May 10, 1961, p. 1; May 29, 1961, p. 1; and June 27, 1961, pp. 1 and 7.

[45] *Sidney Review,* June 27, 1961, p. 1 and 7.

[46] *Sidney Review,* August 2, 1961, p. 1 and 10.

[47] *Sidney Review,* August 30, 1961, p. 8.

[48] O. New, Gulf Island Navigation Ltd., to Provincial Cabinet, brief, October 1961, Legislative Library, Parliament Buildings, Victoria.

[49] *Sidney Review,* November 1, 1961, p. 1, and interview with O. New, June 1982.

[50] *Sidney Review,* August 2, 1962, p. 1.

[51] British Columbia *Department of Highways Reports,* 1955-1959. (Victoria: Queen's Printer, 1955-1959.)

[52] *Sidney Review,* April 18, 1962, p. 1. Mayne Island had 56 taxpayers in 1941 and 225 taxpayers in 1961. The farms of David Bennett, Jack Aitken and Dalton Deacon were sold to real estate developers from the mainland, and to one local entrepreneur from Galiano.

[53] *Sidney Review,* December 20, 1961, p. 7.

[54] *Sidney Review,* April 16, 1958, p. 1.

[55] *Sidney Review,* July 15, 1959, pp. 1 and 8.

[56] A. Davidson, H. B. Peach and D. J. Ferrie, "Upper Cretaceous and Tertiary Sediments, Eastern Vancouver Island and Gulf Islands, British Columbia," Report of Field Party 258, 1963, Shell Canada Limited, October 1965, Shell Canada Limited, Calgary Alberta; and Roger Stickney to author, March 27, 1978.

[57] Interview with Fred and Margaret Bennett, November 1981.

[58] Walter G. Hardwick developed his geographical term Georgia Strait urban region in "The Georgia Strait Urban Region," *British Columbia,* ed. J. Lewis Robinson (Toronto: University of Toronto Press, 1972), pp. 121-133.

CHAPTER V

[1] F. Bosselman and D. Callie, *The Quiet Revolution in Land Use Control* (Washington, D. C.: Council on Environmental Quality, 1971), pp. 1-4; Julia Mary Glover, "The Islands Trust Concept" (Master of Science thesis, University of British Columbia, 1974), 191.

[2] James D. McRae, *The Influence of Exurbanite Settlement on Rural Areas: A Review of the Canadian Literature,* Lands Directorate, Environment Canada, Working Paper No. 3 (Ottawa: Queen's Printer, 1980), pp. 4-6.

[3] Edward M. Gibson, *The Urbanization of the Strait of Georgia Region,* Lands Directorate, Environment of Canada, Paper No. 57 (Ottawa: Queen's Printer, 1976), p. 22; Canada, Dominion Bureau of Statistics, *1951 Census of Canada,* 6:86, and *1976 Census of Canada,* 3:43-44.

[4] The idea of a vacation home within easy commuting distance of the city is not new. European countries, especially Sweden and France, were enjoying this arrangement much earlier in the century, as well as the wealthy families of the eastern United States and Canada. See: Hugh D. Clout, "The Growth of Second-Home Ownership: an Example of Seasonal Suburbanization," in James H. Johnston ed., *Suburban Growth* (London: John Wiley & Sons, 1974), pp. 101-127.

[5] Vancouver *Province,* July 4, 1963, p. 1.

[6] *Sidney Review,* July 24, 1963, p. 1, and September 18, 1963, p. 1.

[7] *Vancouver Sun,* August 29, 1968, p. 12; communication from B. C. Ferry Corporation, Victoria, May 26, 1982, and January 10, 1984.

[8] Capital Regional District Planning Department, *Gulf Islands Study* (Victoria: 1970), p. 3.

[9] Islands Trust, *Some Basic Statistical Data for the Designated Islands (As of April 1978)* (Victoria 1978), unpaginated.

[10] Moira Farrow, "Gulf Islands Become a Gold Mine," *Vancouver Sun,* August 29, 1968, p. 12. Information about Village Bay subdivision was obtained from a newspaper clipping in the possession of Frank Cotton, Mayne Island, undated and untitled, and from an interview with one of the original owners of a lot in the subdivision, Mrs. Bertha Evans, Mayne Island, January 1982.

[11] Jim Hume, "Gulf Paradise Doomed — Islands Jammed Within 10 Years," *Victoria Daily Times,* November 1, 1969, pp. 1-2 and p. 40.

[12] Jess Odam, "Gulf Islands at the Crossroads; Water Wonderland or Just Another Suburb?", *Vancouver Sun,* December 7, 1951, p. 39.

[13] Hume, *Victoria Daily Times,* November 1, 1969, p. 1; *Victoria Daily Times,* June 21, 1971, p. 17, and Vancouver *Province,* August 9, 1972, p. 4. Also, Islands Trust, *Some Basic Statistical Data,* unpaginated. By the time that the Islands Trust published their survey of land ownership in April 1978, only 398 parcels, or 1.5% of all the land in the 13 major islands, was owned by American investors. The Trust did not investigate ownership of the very small islets in Georgia Strait and quite possibly many of these were in American hands.

[14] Robert W. Collier, "The Evolution of Regional Districts in British Columbia," *B. C. Studies* 15 (Autumn, 1972), 29-33.

[15] Ibid., p. 33.

[16] Capital Regional District, *Corporate Structure of the Capital Regional District, 1961.* (Small pamphlet, unpaginated.)

[17] Ibid., and Michael Bennett, Planning Assistant, Capital Regional District, Victoria, interview, January 1982.

[18] Glover, "The Islands Trust Concept," p. 18, and Michael Bennett, interview, January 1982.

[19] Glover, "The Islands Trust Concept," p. 19.

[20] Glover, "The Islands Trust Concept," p. 20; Jess Odam, "Water Wonderland," *Vancouver Sun,* December 7, 1971, p. 39; Peter McNelly, "Campbell's 'Crude Tool' Works to Get Planning for Beauty Spots," *Victoria Daily Times,* May 2, 1970, p. 18.

[21] "Campbell Hardens Line on Gulf Island Land Use," *Victoria Daily Times,* January 6, 1970, p. 13.

[22] Ibid.

[23] Michael Bennett, interview January 1982, and *Sidney Review,* January 14, 1970, p. 7.

[24] *Sidney Review,* April 1, 1970, p. 1.

[25] "Gulf Islands Said Main Issue Facing Capital Region Today," *Victoria Daily Times,* January 22, 1970, p. 19.

[26] *Sidney Review,* April 1, 1970, p. 1.

[27] Capital Regional District, *Gulf Islands Options,* (Victoria: 1971).

[28] *Colonist,* September 5, 1971, p. 13.

[29] *Gulf Islands Options.* The fixed link proposal gained publicity again in 1980 when Dr. Pat McGeer, proposed a route starting at Roberts Bank, across Georgia Strait to Galiano Island, Valdes, Gabriola and Vancouver Island. Alan Daniels, "McGeer envisions link with floating bridges, marinas, port facilities," *Vancouver Sun,* May 27, 1980, p. A17. Three pre-feasibility studies were completed for McGeer's Ministry of Universities, Science and Communications in July and August 1980. See Willis, Cunlifffe, Tait & Company Ltd., "A Floating Bridge From Vancouver Island to the Mainland"; Parsons Brinckerhoff Inc., "Conceptual Report: The Strait of Georgia Fixed-Link Crossing"; and Fenco-Lanmer, "Strait of Georgia Fixed Crossing." Estimates for the crossing ranged from $50,000 million to $4 billion.

[30] *Gulf Islands Options.*

[31] Ibid.

[32] Ibid.

[33] Capital Regional District, *Summary of Gulf Islands Questionnaires Received to April 15, 1972* (Victoria: 1972.)

[34] Ibid.

[35] Interview with Michael Bennett, January 1982. The regional plan was never formally adopted by the CRD.

[36] *Vancouver Sun,* May 15, 1972, p. 10; and August 18, 1972, p. 11.

[37] Glover, "The Islands Trust Concept," pp. 28-30; "MLAs Urge Stiff Clamps on Gulf Islands' Affairs," *Victoria Times,* September 25, 1973; and "Campbell Tees Off," *Victoria Times,* September 15, 1973, p. 2.

[38] *Vancouver Sun,* July 4, 1973, p. 10.

[39] "MLAs Urge Stiff Clamps," *Victoria Times,* September 25, 1973, p. 23; and *Proceedings,* Legislative Assembly of British Columbia, September 24, 1973, pp. 2-4. See Also Glover, "The Islands Trust Concept," pp.31-32.

[40] *Proceedings,* September 24, 1973, pp. 3-4.

[41] *Victoria Times,* September 27, 1973, p. 16.

[42] Glover cites in "The Islands Trust Concept," the U. S. Congress Nantucket Sound Islands Trust Bill 1975, the Hawaii Land Use Law of 1961 as amended 1970, and the Niagara Escarpment Planning and Development Act, 1973. pp. ii-iii.

[43] "Story of Island Plans Outlined at Meeting," *Gulf Islands Driftwood,* December 16, 1981, p. 14.

[44] *Vancouver Province,* June 6, 1974, p. 11; Islands Trust Act, 4 (1) 1979 (R.S. Ch. 208).

[45] Barbara McLintock, "Islands Trust Act Carries Big Stick," *Vancouver Province,* April 25, 1974, pp. 13-14.

[46] Barbara McLintock, "Islands Trust Act," *Vancouver Province,* April 25, 1974, pp. 31, and *Vancouver Province,* May 22, 1974, pp. 13-14.

[47] "Plans for Islands Trust Paternalism — Campbell," *Vancouver Province,* April 26, 1974, p. 9.

[48] "Gulf Islanders Pledged Voice in Future," *Vancouver Province,* September 12, 1974, p. 29.

[49] G. S. Humphreys, Ganges, to *Victoria Times,* November 3, 1973, p. 23

[50] Observation of author at public meeting attended by Hugh Curtis, May 1974, Mayne Island.

[51] *Victoria Times,* May 20, 1977, p. 6, and June 22, 1977, p. 12; *Vancouver Sun,* March 12, 1977, p. 13, and July 15, 1977, p. 80; "Amended Bill Slammed by Opposition Critics," *Vancouver Sun,* September 1, 1979, p. 7; and *Victoria Times,* September 16, 1978, p. 6.

[52] *Victoria Times,* September 16, 1978, p. 6.

[53] Islands Trust Regional Plan (Victoria, 1982), p. 6. This plan has not been adopted by the provincial government, and therefore remains a policy statement, only.

[54] Moira Farrow, "Island Residents Upset by Dock Across Beach," *Vancouver Sun,* August 20, 1979, p. A9.

[55] Laura Kathryn Porcher, "The Islands Trust: An Institutional Experiment in the Management of Scarce Natural and Social Resources" (Master of Science thesis, University of British Columbia, 1980), pp. 123-129.

[56] Porcher, "Islands Trust," pp. 144-146; interview with Joan Sprague, Mayne Island, formerly co-chairman of the Bennett Bay Preservation Committee, now Mayne Island Trust representative, January 1982; and Farrow, "Island Residents," *Vancouver Sun,* August 20, 1979, p. A9. There were 124/201 written and 17/27 oral submissions against Pinchin Holdings' dock.

[57] "Island Trust Defied Over Floats," *Victoria Times,* June 7, 1979, p. 19.

[58] Seaton, Reasons for Judgment, Victoria Registry No. 142/81, p. 7; and Porcher, "Islands Trust," pp. 146-149.

[59] Ibid.

[60] Porcher, "Islands Trust," pp. 161-162; and "The Islands Trust Explained," *The Islands,* 1, December 1982, 8.

[61] Moira Farrow, "Gambier Open Pit Mine Project Draws Opposition," *Vancouver Sun,* September 25, 1979, p. 13A. The article states that "This company . . . has staked nearly three-quarter of Gambier in its first venture into mining exploration. Involved is a total of more than 17,000 acres," which suggests all this acreage is on Gambier. The acreage for Gambier is given as 14,400 in *Islands Trust, Some Basic Statistical Data for the Designated Islands* (As of April 1978.) Islands Trust, Victoria, has advised that 12,000 acres are involved. (John Rich to author, June 1982.)

[62] John Rich, statement, Mayne Island, May 15, 1982; and William Miller, "Islands Trust Hits Secrecy on Route," *Times-Colonist,* December 16, 1981, p. 10.

[63] W. N. English, "Use Conflict in Marine Conservation in the Straits of Georgia," in *Coastal Zone,* 1, Selected Background Papers (Ottawa: Environment Canada, 1972), pp. 33-36. Mike Humphries, "Is the Strait of Georgia Becoming a Toilet Bowl?", *The Islands,* 1, January 1982, 5; "Pollution in the Strait of Georgia," *The Islands,* 1, December 1982, 3.

[64] John Rich, "Completing the Trust," *The Islands,* 1, January 1982, 1.

[65] Interview with Joan Sprague, January 1982; interview with David Strongitharm, planner for Mayne Island, Islands Trust, Victoria, January 1982; and *Islands Trust Regional Background Report,* April 1980, p. 85.

[66] Mount Baker is disproved as a source of water in Stickney, "Sedimentology, Stratigraphy and Structure," p. 203. Interview with Ed Williams, December 1981; interview with Dave Potter, Health Inspector for the CRD, Victoria, May 1982; and telephone communication with Groundwater Division, Water Resources Branch, Victoria, May 1982. See also J. C. Foweraker, *Groundwater Investigations on Mayne Island, Report No. 1;* J. Heisterman, *Report No. 2;* and M. C. Moncur, *Report No. 3* (Victoria: Water Investigations Branch, British Columbia Water Resources Service, Dept. of Lands, Forests and Water Resources, 1974.) Technical details regarding fault lines and sedimentary formations should be compared with the more recent scholarship of Stickney, "Sedimentology Stratigraphy and Structure of the Late Cretaceous Rocks of Mayne and Samuel Islands."

[67] Islands Trust meeting at Mayne Island, May 15, 1982, attended by author; and telephone conversation with RCMP, Pender Island, January 1984.

[68] "Islands Trust dies under revised bill," *Times-Colonist,* July 24, 1982, p. 11.

[69] *Times-Colonist,* July 27, 1982, p. 9; July 29, 1982, p. 3; and July 31, 1982, pp. 4 and 5. See also John Mika to Editor, August 8, 1982, *Gulf Islands Driftwood,* August 18, 1982, p. 6. The Trust Council consists of all 26 trustees, who meet informally, quarterly, to consider the problems of mutual concern. "An Introduction to the Islands Trust, 1982," pamphlet, (Victoria: 1982).

[70] Hon. Bill Ritchie, Minister of Municipal Affairs, to author, June 28, 1983.

[71] "An Introduction to the Islands Trust," 1982, pamphlet.

[72] McRae, *The Influence of Exurbanite Settlement,* p. 15.

[73] *Vancouver Province,* March 19, 1966, p. 31; *Sidney Review,* May 27, 1965, p. 1; and "History of MIRA" on file at Mayne Island Museum.

[74] "History of Mayne Island Health Centre," on file at Mayne Island Museum.

[75] Marie Elliott, "Plumper Pass Lockup and Mayne Island Museum," (Victoria: Mayne Island Agricultural Society, 1981), pp. 8-9.

[76] Interview with Miss Foye Miles, warden, St. Mary Magdalene Church, Mayne Island, January 1982.

[77] Statistics Canada census information as quoted in *Islands Trust Regional Plan,* p. 13.

[78] *Islands Trust Regional Plan,* p. 32.

CHAPTER VI

[1] This analogy is suggested by the oft-quoted statement made by Professor H. P. R. Finberg, former head of the Department of Local History, University College, Leicester, that the family, the local community, the national state and the supra-national society can be regarded as a series of concentric circles, the inner circles just as important as the outer ones.

[2] Ormsby, *British Columbia,* p. 107.

INDEX

148